International Airline Phrase Book

IN SIX LANGUAGES

ENGLISH, FRENCH, GERMAN, ITALIAN,
PORTUGUESE AND SPANISH

by

Joseph W. Bátor, Ph.D.

Dover Publications, Inc.
New York

Published in Canada by General Publishing Company, Ltd.,
30 Lesmill Road, Don Mills, Toronto, Ontario.
Published in the United Kingdom by Constable and Company,
Ltd., 10 Orange Street, London WC 2.

International Airline Phrase Book is a new work,
published for the first time by
Dover Publications, Inc., in 1968.

Library of Congress Catalog Card Number: 67-25870

Manufactured in the United States of America

Dover Publications, Inc.
180 Varick Street
New York, N.Y. 10014

To my daughters Alexandra and Ilona
With love, Papa

Preface

The *International Airline Phrase Book* is designed to be used by passengers, airline employees and travel agents in the United States and abroad. The book has a dual purpose: to indicate *what* to say and to indicate *how* to say it.

English is the "anchor" language in the 700 numbered sentences and phrases. Each English sentence is followed by translations (or idiomatic equivalents) in French, German, Italian, Portuguese and Spanish, in that order, signaled by the abbreviations F, G, I, P and S, respectively.

Synonyms are indicated in parentheses. For example, "Clase Económica (OR Turista)." Parentheses are also used to show the feminine form of adjectives, when necessary. For example, "Je suis désolé (FEM. désolée)" indicates that "désolée" is the proper form when a woman is speaking; similarly "Poderei servi-lo (TO FEM. servi-la)?" indicates that "servi-la" is the proper form when a woman is being addressed.

Square brackets indicate a substitution; the words they enclose can be substituted for the immediately preceding word or words, or other applicable words as needed, permitting the formation of new sentences in new situations. For example, the entry "Quali paesi [Quali città] Le piacerebbe visitare?" yields the two sentences "Quali paesi Le piacerebbe visitare?" and "Quali città Le piacerebbe visitare?"

The very complete Index (in English only) will aid the reader in finding the specific words or topics he needs.

Contents

Sommaire

Inhalt

Tabella

Sumário

Sumario

Reservations (or Bookings)

F: RÉSERVATIONS
G: RESERVIERUNGEN (OR BUCHUNGEN)
I: PRENOTAZIONI
P: RESERVAS
S: RESERVACIONES

1. May I help you (OR What can I do for you)?
F: Que puis-je pour vous?
G: Was kann ich für Sie tun (OR Womit kann ich Ihnen dienen)?
I: Posso aiutarLa (OR Cosa posso fare per Lei)?
P: Em que posso ser-lhe útil?
S: ¿En qué puedo servirle?

2. I would like to go to ———.
F: Je désire aller à (OR en*) ———.
G: Ich möchte gerne nach ——— fahren (OR reisen, fliegen).
I: Vorrei andare a (OR in†) ———.
P: Eu pretendo ir para ———.
S: Me gustaría ir a ———.

3. I want to take a trip to ———.
F: Je veux faire un voyage à (OR en*) ———.
G: Ich möchte gerne eine Reise nach ——— machen.
I: Voglio fare un viaggio a (OR in†) ———.
P: Eu quero fazer uma viagem para ———.
S: Me gustaría hacer un viaje a ———.

4. Where do you intend to travel?
F: Où avez-vous l'intention d'aller?

---

* Before names of cities, use à; before names of continents and most countries, use en.
† Before names of cities, use a; before names of continents and countries, in is generally used.

1

G: Wohin beabsichtigen Sie zu reisen?
I: Dove intende viaggiare?
P: Para onde deseja viajar?
S: ¿A dónde piensa viajar?

5. **Around the world; across Europe, to the Far East, to the Near East, to South America, to Africa, to Australia.**

F: Je veux faire le tour du monde; je veux aller à travers l'Europe, en Extrême-Orient, en Proche-Orient, en Amérique du Sud, en Afrique, en Australie.
G: Rund um die Welt; durch Europa, in den Fernen Osten, in den Nahen Osten, nach Südamerika, nach Afrika, nach Australien.
I: Intorno al mondo; attraverso l'Europa, in Estremo Oriente, in Medio Oriente, in America del Sud, in Africa, in Australia.
P: À volta do mundo; pela Europa, pelo Extremo Oriente, pelo Próximo Oriente, pela América do Sud, pela África, pela Austrália.
S: Alrededor del mundo; por Europa, al Lejano Oriente, al Cercano Oriente, a la América del Sur, a África, a Australia.

6. **How much time do you have at your disposal?**

F: De combien de temps disposez-vous?
G: Wieviel Zeit haben Sie zur Verfügung?
I: Quanto tempo ha a Sua disposizione?
P: De quanto tempo pode dispôr para a sua viagem?
S: ¿De cuánto tiempo dispone?

7. **What countries [What cities] would you like to visit?**

F: Quels sont les pays [Quelles sont les villes] que vous désirez visiter?
G: Welche Länder [Welche Städte] möchten Sie gerne sehen (OR besichtigen)?
I: Quali paesi [Quali città] Le piacerebbe visitare?
P: Que países [Que cidades] pretende (OR quer) visitar?
S: ¿Cuáles países [Cuáles ciudades] le gustaría visitar?

8. When would yóu like to commence your trip?
F: Quand désirez-vous partir?
G: Wann möchten Sie Ihre Reise beginnen?
I: Quando vuole cominciare il Suo viaggio?
P: Quando quer começar a sua viagem?
S: ¿Cuándo le gustaría comenzar su viaje?

9. We want to leave for ———— next Friday.
F: Nous désirons partir pour ———— vendredi prochain.
G: Wir möchten am nächsten Freitag nach ————
abfliegen.
I: Vogliamo andare a (OR in) ———— venerdì prossimo.
P: Nós queremos partir para ———— na próxima sexta-
feira.
S: Queremos salir para ———— el próximo viernes.

10. How many passengers will be traveling with you?
F: Combien de passagers êtes-vous?
G: Wieviel Personen sind Sie?
I: Quanti passeggeri viaggeranno con Lei?
P: Quantas pessoas viajarão consigo?
S: ¿Cuántos pasajeros irán con Ud.?

11. Are you traveling alone?
F: Voyagez-vous seul?
G: Reisen Sie allein?
I: Viaggerà da solo?
P: Viaja só?
S: ¿Viaja sólo?

12. No, I will be traveling with my family.
F: Non, je voyage avec ma famille.
G: Nein, ich reise mit meiner Familie.
I: No, viaggerò con la mia famiglia.
P: Não, vou viajar com a minha família.
S: No, viajo con mi familia.

13. I need [four] seats, Economy Class.
F: Je désire [quatre] places en Classe Économique.
G: Ich benötige (OR brauche) [vier] Plätze, Touristen-klasse.
I: Ho bisogno di [quattro] posti in Classe Economica.
P: Eu quero marcar [quatro] lugares em Classe Económica.
S: Necesito [cuatro] asientos (OR plazas), Clase Ecónomica (OR Turista).

14. Just a moment, please. I am going to check.
F: Un instant, s'il vous plaît, je vais vérifier.
G: Einen Moment (OR Einen Augenblick) bitte, ich werde nachsehen.
I: Un momento, prego, controllerò.
P: Um momento, por favor, vou verificar.
S: Un momento, por favor, voy a averiguar.

15. I am sorry, but on this flight there are no more seats available in Economy Class.
F: Je suis désolé (FEM. désolée), mais ce vol est complet en Classe Économique.
G: Ich bedauere, aber für diesen Flug gibt es in der Touristenklasse keine freien Plätze mehr.
I: Mi dispiace, ma non ci sono più posti disponibili in Economica su questo volo.
P: Tenho pena, mas já não temos lugares para este vôo em Classe Económica.
S: Lo siento, pero no quedan más asientos (OR plazas) libres en este vuelo en Clase Económica.

16. I can confirm First Class on that day. Of course, the price is higher.
F: Je peux vous confirmer des places en Première Classe pour cette date, mais le prix sera plus élevé.
G: Ich könnte Ihren Flug an diesem Tag in der Ersten Klasse buchen. Natürlich kostet die Erste Klasse mehr.

I: Posso confermare la Prima Classe per quel giorno. Naturalmente il prezzo è più alto.

P: Posso confirmá-los em Primeira Classe para esse dia. Certamente em Primeira Classe é mais caro.

S: Puedo confirmarle en Primera Clase para ese día. Desde luego el precio es mayor.

17. What is the difference between First Class and Economy Class?

F: Quelle est la différence entre Première Classe et Classe Économique?

G: Was ist der Unterschied zwischen der Ersten und der Touristenklasse?

I: Qual'è la differenza fra Prima Classe e Economica?

P: Qual é a diferença entre a Primeira Classe e a Classe Económica?

S: ¿Cuál es la diferencia entre Primera Clase y Clase Económica?

18. In First Class the seating is more comfortable.

F: En Première Classe vous êtes assuré (TO FEM. assurée) de plus de confort.

G: In der Ersten Klasse sind die Sitze viel bequemer.

I: In Prima Classe il posto è più comodo.

P: Na Primeira Classe os lugares são mais confortáveis.

S: En Primera Clase el asiento es más cómodo.

19. Your baggage allowance is ——— pounds, or ——— kilos.

F: Votre franchise de bagage est de ——— livres, ou ——— kilos.

G: Sie können ——— Pfund, oder ——— Kilo, mitnehmen.

I: Il suo bagaglio potrà essere di ——— libbre, o ——— chili.

P: Pode transportar ——— libras, ou ——— quilos.

S: El peso de equipaje permitido es de ——— libras, o ——— kilos.

20. You also have complimentary drinks and a variety of dishes.

F: Les boissons et les menus sont à volonté et à votre choix.

G: Außerdem sind die Getränke frei und Sie haben eine Auswahl an Gerichten.

I: Le sarà inoltre offerto da bere ed una varietà di piatti.

P: Além disso são servidas gratuitamente bebidas e uma grande variedade de pratos.

S: También tiene bebidas gratuitas y una variedad de platos.

21. In Economy Class your baggage allowance is ——— pounds, or ——— kilos.

F: En Classe Économique la franchise de bagage est de ——— livres, ou ——— kilos.

G: In der Touristenklasse können Sie ——— Pfund, oder ——— Kilo, mitnehmen.

I: In Classe Economica il suo bagaglio potrà essere di ——— libbre, o ——— chili.

P: Na Classe Económica pode transportar ——— libras, ou ——— quilos.

S: En Clase Económica el peso de equipaje permitido es de ——— libras, o ——— kilos.

22. I do not want to travel First Class. It is too expensive for me.

F: Je ne désire pas voyager en Première Classe. Le prix est trop élevé.

G: Ich möchte nicht Erster Klasse fliegen, es ist mir zu teuer.

I: Non voglio viaggiare in Prima Classe. Costa troppo per me.

P: Não quero ir em Primeira Classe. É muito caro para mim.

S: No quiero viajar en Primera Clase. Es demasiado caro.

23. **I will take the [four] Economy Class seats on your Flight Number ——— on Sunday as you recommended.**

F: Je prendrai les [quatre] places en Classe Économique sur le vol numéro ——— dimanche comme vous me le recommandez.

G: Ich möchte die [vier] Plätze in der Touristenklasse auf Ihrem Flug Nummer ——— am Sonntag nehmen, wie Sie es mir empfohlen haben.

I: Prenderò i [quattro] posti in Classe Economica sul volo numero ——— di domenica come mi avete raccomandato.

P: Prefiro os [quatro] lugares em Classe Económica no vosso vôo número ——— no Domingo como me recomendou.

S: Tomaré los [cuatro] asientos (OR las [cuatro] plazas) en Clase Económica en su vuelo número ——— del domingo como Ud. me recomendó.

24. **Your reservation is now confirmed on Flight Number ———, Economy Class.**

F: Votre réservation est confirmée sur le vol numéro ——— en Classe Économique.

G: Ihre Reservierung ist auf Flug Nummer ——— in der Touristenklasse bestätigt.

I: La Sua prenotazione è confermata sul volo numero ——— in Classa Economica.

P: A sua reserva fica confirmada para o vôo número ——— em Classe Económica.

S: Su reservación está confirmada para el vuelo número ——— en Clase Económica.

25. **On Sunday, February fifteenth (15), departing from [Boston] at [ten] o'clock a.m. [p.m.], local time.**

F: Dimanche, le quinze (15) février, décollage de [Boston] à [dix] heures du matin [de l'après-midi; du soir], heure locale.

G: Am Sonntag, den fünfzehnten (15.) Februar, Abflug von [Boston] um [zehn] Uhr morgens [nachmittags; abends], Ortszeit.

I: Domenica, il quindici (15) febbraio, in partenza da [Boston] alle [dieci] di mattina [del pomeriggio; di sera], ora locale.

P: No Domingo, dia quinze (15) de Fevereiro, com partida de [Boston] às [dez] horas da manhã [da tarde], horas locais.

S: El domingo, quince (15) de Febrero, partiendo de [Boston] a las [diez] de la mañana [de la tarde], hora local.

26. May I have the spelling of your family name (OR last name) [your given name (OR first name)]?

F: Voulez-vous m'épeler votre nom de famille [votre prénom]?

G: Würden Sie mir bitte Ihren Familiennamen [Ihren Vornamen] buchstabieren?

I: Vuole sillabarmi il cognome [il nome], prego?

P: Pode dizer-me por letras o seu apelido [o seu nome próprio]?

S: ¿Quiere deletrearme su apellido [su nombre]?

27. Would you prefer to leave your home or your business telephone number?

F: Préférez-vóus me donner votre numéro de téléphone personnel ou le numéro de bureau?

G: Würden Sie mir lieber Ihre Privattelephonnummer oder Ihre Büronummer zurücklassen?

I: Preferisce lasciare il numero di telefono di casa o quello dell'ufficio?

P: Prefere dar-me o telefone da sua casa ou o do seu escritório?

S: ¿Prefiere dejar el número de teléfono de su casa o el de su oficina?

28. May I also have your home or business address?
  F: Puis-je aussi avoir votre adresse personnelle ou de bureau?
  G: Darf ich auch um Ihre Privat- oder Geschäftsanschrift (OR Geschäftsadresse) bitten?
  I: Posso avere anche il Suo indirizzo di casa o d'ufficio?
  P: Pode dar-me também a sua morada ou endereço do escritório?
  S: ¿Podría decirme su domicilio o la dirección de su oficina?

29. Why do you need my telephone number and my address?
  F: Pourquoi désirez-vous mon numéro de téléphone et mon adresse?
  G: Warum brauchen Sie meine Telephonnummer und meine Adresse?
  I: Perchè ha bisogno del mio numero di telefono e indirizzo?
  P: Porquê é que precisa do meu telefone e da minha morada?
  S: ¿Por qué necesita mi número de teléfono y mi dirección?

30. In case of necessity, we want to notify you, Sir, or leave a message for you.
  F: En cas de nécessité nous désirons vous prévenir, Monsieur, ou vous laisser un message.
  G: Gegebenenfalls werden wir Sie verständigen oder Ihnen eine Nachricht hinterlassen.
  I: In caso di necessità, vogliamo notificarLa, Signore, o lasciare un messaggio per Lei.
  P: Em caso de necessidade, nós queremos avisá-lo ou deixar-lhe recado.
  S: En caso de necesidad, queremos notificarle o dejarle un mensaje.

31. In case of any change in departure time that might occur due to bad weather.

F: En cas de changement de votre heure de départ occasionné par le mauvais temps.

G: Falls sich die Abflugzeit wegen schlechten Wetters ändert.

I: In caso di cambiamento dell'orario di partenza per cattivo tempo.

P: No caso de qualquer alteração da hora da partida que por acaso aconteça devido a mau tempo.

S: En caso de que tengamos cambio en la hora de salida que podría ocurrir debido al mal tiempo.

32. Is there anything else we can do for you?

F: Puis-je vous être d'une autre utilité?

G: Können wir sonst noch etwas für Sie tun?

I: Possiamo fare altro per Lei?

P: Mais alguma coisa em que eu possa ser-lhe útil?

S: ¿Podemos servirle en algo más?

33. Could you recommend some tourist guides [some books on Europe]?

F: Pouvez-vous me recommander des guides touristiques [des livres sur l'Europe]?

G: Welche Reiseführer [Bücher] über Europa können Sie mir empfehlen?

I: Può raccomandare qualche guida turistica [qualche libro sull'Europa]?

P: Poderá indicar-me alguns guías turísticos [alguns livros sobre a Europa]?

S: ¿Podría recomendar algunas guías turísticas [algunos libros sobre Europa]?

34. Certainly, I would suggest you buy ———, which costs only ———.

F: Certainement, je peux vous suggérer d'acheter ———, qui coûte seulement ———.

G: Natürlich, ich würde Ihnen vorschlagen, ——— zu kaufen. Es kostet nur ———.

I: Certo, Le suggerirei di comprare ———, che costa solo ———.

P: Com certeza, recomendar-lhe-ia que comprasse o livro intitulado ———, que custa apenas ———.

S: Ciertamente, le sugiero que compre ———, que solamente cuesta ———.

35. If you read this book carefully before you leave, you will become acquainted with those countries.

F: Si vous lisez ce livre attentivement avant de partir, vous pourrez avoir une idée assez exacte de ces pays.

G: Wenn Sie dieses Buch vor Ihrer Abreise gründlich lesen, werden Sie die betreffenden Länder schon gut kennen.

I: Leggendo con cura questo libro prima di partire, Lei farà conoscenza con questi paesi.

P: Se ler este livro com cuidado antes da sua partida, estes países tornar-se-ão seus conhecidos.

S: Si lee cuidadosamente este libro antes de la salida, se habrá familiarizado con esos países.

36. I also have some illustrated folders on several countries for you.

F: Je possède encore pour votre usage des dépliants illustrés sur plusieurs pays.

G: Außerdem habe ich für Sie einige Bildprospekte über verschiedene andere Länder.

I: Ho anche degli opuscoli illustrati su molti paesi per Lei.

P: Também tenho alguns folhetos ilustrados sobre vários países.

S: También tengo folletos ilustrados sobre diferentes países.

37. Thanks for your reservation, and enjoy your trip!

F: Je vous remercie de votre réservation et je vous souhaite un bon voyage!

G: Vielen Dank für Ihre Buchung. Ich wünsche Ihnen
eine gute Reise!

I: Grazie per la prenotazione e buon viaggio!

P: Muito obrigado (FEM. obrigada) por ter preferido os
nossos serviços. Desejamos-lhe muito boa viagem.

S: ¡Gracias por su reservación y disfrute de su viaje!

38. **To another customer: Will you be so kind as to have a
seat?**

F: *À un autre client:* Voulez-vous vous asseoir?

G: *Zu einem anderen Kunden:* Würden Sie bitte Platz
nehmen?

I: *Ad un nuovo cliente:* Vuole accomodarsi, prego?

P: *A um novo cliente:* Quer ter a bondade de se sentar?

S: *A un nuevo cliente:* ¿Quiere tomar asiento, por favor?

39. **I shall be with you as soon as I have taken care of this
passenger.**

F: Dès que j'aurai fini avec ce passager, je serai à votre
disposition.

G: Ich werde Sie sofort bedienen, sobald ich mit diesem
Passagier fertig bin.

I: Sarò da Lei appena finito con questo passeggero.

P: Atendê-lo-ei logo que este cliente esteja despachado.

S: Le atenderé tan pronto como haya terminado con este
pasajero.

40. **Will you be traveling First Class or Economy Class?**

F: Voyagez-vous en Première Classe ou en Classe
Économique?

G: Möchten Sie in der Ersten- oder in der Touristenklasse
fliegen?

I: Viaggerà in Prima Classe o in Economica?

P: Viaja em Primeira Classe ou em Classe Económica?

S: ¿Viajará en Primera Clase o en Económica?

41. **When do you plan to return?**

F: Quand pensez-vous retourner?

G: Wann wollen Sie zurückreisen?
I: Quando prevede di tornare?
P: Quando pensa regressar?
S: ¿Cuándo piensa regresar?

42. How long do you wish to stay in ———?
F: Combien de temps désirez-vous passer à (OR en) ———?
G: Wie lange möchten Sie in ——— bleiben?
I: Quanto tempo desidera rimanere a (OR in) ———?
P: Quanto tempo quer ficar em ———?
S: ¿Cuánto tiempo desea permanecer en ———?

43. How much will this trip cost me?
F: Combien ce voyage va-t-il coûter?
G: Wieviel wird mich diese Reise kosten?
I: Quanto mi costerà questo viaggio?
P: Quanto me vai custar esta viagem?
S: ¿Cuánto me costará este viaje?

44. At the time you plan to travel, we have a special excursion fare.
F: Pour l'époque de votre voyage, nous avons un tarif spécial d'excursion.
G: In der Zeit Ihrer geplanten Reise ist der Tarif ermäßigt.
I: Per l'epoca che progetta di viaggiare, abbiamo un prezzo speciale d'escursione.
P: Na altura em que pensa viajar nós temos uma tarifa especial de excursão.
S: Para cuando Ud. planea viajar, tenemos tarifa de excursión.

45. How many times a week do you have a flight from ——— to ———?
F: Quelles sont les fréquences par semaine de vos vols entre ——— et ———?

G: Wieviel Flüge haben Sie wöchentlich von ———
nach ———?

I: Quante volte alla settimana avete un volo da ——— a
———?

P: Quantas vezes por semana têm vôos de ——— para
———?

S: ¿Cuántos vuelos tienen por semana desde ——— a
———?

46. We have a daily flight from ——— to ———.
F: Nous avons un vol quotidien entre ——— et ———.
G: Wir fliegen täglich von ——— nach ———.
I: Abbiamo un volo giornaliero da ——— a ———.
P: Nós temos um vôo diário de ——— para ———.
S: Tenemos un vuelo diario desde ——— a ———.

47. Once [twice; three times] a week, on Mondays, Wednesdays and Sundays.
F: Une fois [deux fois; trois fois] la semaine, le lundi, le mercredi et le dimanche.
G: Einmal [zweimal; dreimal] wöchentlich, montags, mittwochs und sonntags.
I: Una volta [due volte; tre volte] alla settimana, il lunedì, il mercoledì e la domenica.
P: Uma vez [duas vezes; três vezes] por semana, às segundas, quartas e domingos.
S: Una vez [dos veces; tres veces] por semana, los lunes, los miércoles y los domingos.

48. Departing from [Chicago] at [two] o'clock in the morning [in the afternoon].
F: Partant de [Chicago] à [deux] heures du matin [de l'après-midi].
G: Abflug von [Chicago] um [zwei] Uhr morgens [nachmittags].
I: In partenza da [Chicago] alle [due] di mattina [del pomeriggio].

P: Com partida de [Chicago] às [duas] horas da manhã [da tarde].
S: Saliendo de [Chicago] a las [dos] de la mañana [de la tarde].

49. Arriving in [Rome] at [nine] o'clock in the evening.
F: Arrivant à [Rome] à [neuf] heures du soir.
G: Ankunft in [Rom] um [neun] Uhr abends.
I: In arrivo a [Roma] alle [nove] ore della sera.
P: Com chegada a [Roma] às [nove] horas da tarde.
S: Llegando a [Roma] a las [nueve] de la tarde.

50. Do you have a summer [winter] schedule?
F: Avez-vous un horaire d'été [d'hiver]?
G: Haben Sie einen Sommer- [Winter-]Flugplan?
I: Avete un orario estivo [invernale]?
P: Tem um horário de verão [de inverno]?
S: ¿Tiene Ud. un horario de verano [de invierno]?

51. As you see, the number of flights will be considerably increased.
F: Comme vous le constatez, nous augmenterons beaucoup la fréquence de nos vols.
G: Wie Sie daraus ersehen, wird die Anzahl der Flüge beträchtlich erhöht.
I: Come vedete, il numero dei voli sarà considerevolmente aumentato.
P: Como vê, o número de vôos aumentará consideràvelmente.
S: Como Ud. puede ver, el número de los vuelos será aumentado considerablemente.

52. I almost forgot that we also want to visit ———.
F: J'avais presque oublié de vous dire que nous désirons aussi aller à (OR en) ———.
G: Ich hätte beinahe vergessen, daß wir auch nach ——— reisen wollen.

I: Mi stavo dimenticando che noi vogliamo visitare anche ———.

P: Quase me esquecia, também queremos visitar ———.

S: Casi olvidé que también queremos visitar ———.

53. We will take you to ——— and from there we shall arrange the connection.

F: Nous vous transporterons jusqu'à ——— et nous nous chargerons de vous assurer la correspondance.

G: Sie können mit uns bis ——— fliegen und von dortaus werden wir für Sie den Anschluß (OR Weiterflug) arrangieren.

I: Noi vi transporteremo fino a ——— e da lì provvederemo per una coincidenza.

P: Nós levá-lo-emos até ——— e ali arranjaremos uma ligação.

S: Le llevaremos a Ud. a ——— y de ahí arreglaremos su conexión.

54. I would like to continue from ——— to ——— by boat [by train].

F: Je désire me rendre ensuite de ——— à ——— par bateau [par train].

G: Ich möchte meine Reise von ——— nach ——— mit dem Schiff [mit dem Zug] fortsetzen.

I: Desidero proseguire da ——— per ——— in piroscafo [in treno].

P: Eu queria continuar de ——— para ——— de barco [de combóio*].

S: Me gustaría ir de ——— a ——— en barco [en tren].

* In Brazil the word for train is *trem* rather than *combóio*.

Departure (Passengers Checking In)

F: DÉPART (*Enregistrement des passagers*)
G: ABFLUG (*Melden der Passagiere zur Abfertigung*)
I: PARTENZE (*Controllo passeggeri*)
P: PARTIDA (*Processo de passageiros*)
S: PARTIDA (*Proceso de pasajeros*)

Documents

F: DOCUMENTS
G: DOKUMENTE
I: DOCUMENTI
P: DOCUMENTOS
S: DOCUMENTOS

55. Good morning.
F: Bonjour.
G: Guten Morgen.
I: ꞌBuon giorno.
P: Bom dia.
S: Buenos días.

56. Good day.
F: Bonjour.
G: Guten Tag.
I: Buon giorno.
P: Bom dia.
S: Buenos días.

57. Good afternoon.
F: Bonjour.
G: Guten Tag.

I: Buon giorno.
P: Boa tarde.
S: Buenas tardes.

58. Good evening.
F: Bonsoir.
G: Guten Abend.
I: Buona sera.
P: Boa tarde.
S: Buenas tardes.

59. May I see your ticket [your passport]?
F: Permettez-moi de voir votre billet [votre passeport].
G: Darf ich Sie um Ihren Flugschein [Ihren Paß] bitten?
I: Per favore, potrei vedere il Suo biglietto [il Suo passaporto]?
P: Posso ver o seu bilhete [o seu passaporte]?
S: Permítame ver su billete (OR pasaje, boleto*) [su pasaporte].

60. May I see your vaccination certificate?
F: Permettez-moi de voir votre certificat de vaccination.
G: Darf ich Sie um Ihr Impfzeugnis bitten?
I: Potrei vedere il Suo certificato di vaccinazione?
P: Posso ver o seu certificado de vacina?
S: Permítame ver su certificado de vacuna.

61. Are you traveling together?
F: Voyagez-vous ensemble?
G: Reisen Sie zusammen?
I: Viaggiano insieme?
P: Viajam juntos?
S: ¿Viajan juntos?

* "Ticket" is *pasaje* or *boleto* in some parts of South America.

62. Are you a resident of ———?
F: Résidez-vous à (OR en) ———?
G: Wohnen Sie in ———?
I: È Lei residente a (OR in) ———?
P: É residente de ———?
S: ¿Es residente en ———?

63. May I see your resident's card?
F: Puis-je voir votre carte de résidence?
G: Darf ich Sie um Ihre Aufenthaltsgenehmigung bitten?
I: Per favore, potrei vedere la Sua carta di residenza?
P: Posso ver o seu cartão de residência?
S: Permítame ver su tarjeta de residencia.

64. I cannot find my identity card.
F: Je ne trouve pas ma carte d'identité.
G: Ich kann meinen Personalausweis nicht finden.
I: Non riesco a trovare la mia carta d'identità.
P: Não posso encontrar o meu cartão de identidade.
S: No encuentro mi tarjeta (OR cédula) de identidad.

65. I have left it at home.
F: Je l'ai laissée à la maison.
G: Ich habe ihn zu Hause gelassen.
I: L'ho lasciata a casa.
P: Deixei-o em casa.
S: La olvidé en casa.

66. Here is my alien registration card.
F: Voici ma carte de résidence.
G: Hier ist mein Personalausweis für Ausländer.
I: Ecco la mia carta di residenza per stranieri.
P: Aqui está o meu cartão de residência para estrangeiros.
S: Aquí está mi tarjeta de residencia para extranjeros.

67. To a disabled passenger: Is somebody traveling with you?
    F: *À un passager infirme:* Quelqu'un voyage-t-il avec
    vous?
    G: *Zu einem körperbehinderten Passagier:* Reist jemand
    mit Ihnen?
    I: *A un passeggero incapacitato:* C'è qualcuno che
    viaggia con Lei?
    P: *A um passageiro incapacitado:* Viaja alguém consigo?
    S: *A un pasajero incapacitado:* ¿Le acompaña alguien en
    el viaje?

68. Can you walk with a little help?
    F: Pouvez-vous marcher si nous vous aidons?
    G: Können Sie mit einiger Hilfe gehen?
    I: Può camminare con aiuto?
    P: Pode andar com ajuda?
    S: ¿Puede caminar con ayuda?

69. I am going to request a wheelchair.
    F: Je vais demander une chaise roulante.
    G: Ich werde einen Rollstuhl anfordern.
    I: Richiederò per Lei una sedia a rotelle.
    P: Vou pedir uma cadeira de rodas.
    S: Pediré una silla de ruedas.

70. What is your address?
    F: Quelle est votre adresse?
    G: Würden Sie mir Ihre Adresse geben?
    I: Qual'è il Suo indirizzo?
    P: Qual é o seu endereço?
    S: ¿Cuál es su dirección?

71. Are you going as a tourist or on business?
    F: Voyagez-vous comme touriste ou pour affaires?
    G: Sind Sie Tourist oder Geschäftsreisender?
    I: Viaggia per turismo o per affari?
    P: Viaja como turista ou em negócios?
    S: ¿Viaja como turista o de negocios?

72. I am going as a tourist.
F: Je suis touriste.
G: Ich reise als Tourist.
I: Vado come turista.
P: Viajo como turista.'
S: Viajo como turista.

73. Here are my photographs.
F: Voici mes photographies.
G: Hier sind meine Photographien.
I: Ecco le mie fotografie.
P: Aqui estão as minhas fotografias.
S: Aquí están mis fotografías.

74. The employee at the other counter will help you.
F: L'agent de l'autre comptoir va vous aider.
G: Der Angestellte an dem anderen Schalter wird Sie
    bedienen.
I: L'impiegato dell'altro banco L'aiuterà.
P: O empregado no outro balcão o ajudará.
S: El empleado en el otro mostrador le atenderá.

75. This passport has expired.
F: La validité de ce passeport est expirée.
G: Dieser Paß ist ungültig.
I: Questo passaporto è scaduto.
P: A validade deste passaporte já expirou.
S: Este pasaporte está vencido (OR caducado).

76. I'm sorry, but we cannot permit you to travel.
F: Je suis désolé (FEM. désolée), mais nous ne pouvons pas
    vous permettre de voyager.
G: Ich bedauere, aber wir dürfen Sie nicht reisen lassen.
I: Mi dispiace, ma non possiamo farLa partire.
P: Lamento, mas não podemos permitir que viaje.
S: Lo lamentamos mucho, pero no podemos permitirle
    que viaje.

77. You must have this passport renewed.
F: Vous devez faire renouveler ce passeport.
G: Sie müssen diesen Paß verlängern lassen.
I: Lei deve rinnovare questo passaporto.
P: Tem que ter este passaporte renovado.
S: Su pasaporte debe ser renovado.

78. You must get a new passport.
F: Vous devez obtenir un nouveau passeport.
G: Sie müssen sich einen neuen Paß besorgen.
I: Lei deve richiedere un nuovo passaporto.
P: Deve obter um novo passaporte.
S: Tiene que obtener un nuevo pasaporte.

79. We will rewrite (OR reissue) your ticket.
F: Nous allons réémettre votre billet.
G: Wir werden Ihren Flugschein umschreiben (OR neu ausstellen).
I: Dovremo riemettere il Suo biglietto.
P: Reemitiremos o seu bilhete.
S: Tenemos que cambiar su billete (OR boleto, pasaje).

80. I have to revalidate your ticket.
F: Je dois revalider votre billet.
G: Ich muß Ihren Flugschein umbuchen (OR neu eintragen).
I: Devo rivalidare il Suo biglietto.
P: Tenho que revalidar o seu bilhete.
S: Tengo que revalidar su billete.

81. Do you have a visa for ———?
F: Avez-vous un visa pour ———?
G: Haben Sie ein Visum für ———?
I: Ha il visto per ———?
P: Tem visto para ———?
S: ¿Tiene visa (OR visado, visación) para ———?

82. I didn't think I needed one.
F: Je pensais que je n'en avais pas besoin.
G: Ich wußte nicht, daß ich eins brauche.
I: Pensavo che non fosse necessario.
P: Pensei não precisar de um visto.
S: Creía que no la necesitaba.

83. I forgot to get it.
F: J'ai oublié d'en obtenir un.
G: Ich habe vergessen, mir eins zu besorgen.
I: Ho dimenticato di prenderlo.
P: Esqueci-me de o obter.
S: Me olvidé de conseguirla.

84. Sorry, but this is a requirement of the country concerned.
F: Je suis désolé (FEM. désolée), mais c'est la réglementation de ce pays-là.
G: Es tut mir leid, aber das betreffende Land verlangt das.
I: Mi dispiace, ma questo è richiesto dall'autorità del rispettivo paese.
P: Lamento, mas isto é um requerimento do respectivo país.
S: Lamento mucho, pero esto es un requerimiento de dicho país.

85. Can you help me?
F: Pouvez-vous m'aider?
G: Können Sie mir helfen?
I: Mi può aiutare?
P: Pode-me ajudar?
S: ¿Podría ayudarme?

86. You could travel with us to ———.
F: Vous pourriez voyager avec nous jusqu'à ———.
G: Sie könnten mit uns nach ——— fliegen.

I: Lei potrebbe viaggiare con noi fino a ———.
P: Podia viajar connosco* para ———.
S: Ud. podría viajar con nosotros hasta ———.

87. **There you will be able to obtain your visa for** ———.
    F: Vous pourriez obtenir là-bas votre visa pour ———.
    G: Dort kann Ihr Visum für ——— durch den Konsul ausgestellt werden.
    I: Lì può ottenere il visto per ———.
    P: Lá poderá obter o seu visto para ———.
    S: Allí podrá conseguir su visa para ———.

88. **You could continue your trip on the first available flight to** ———.
    F: Vous pourriez continuer votre voyage sur le premier vol disponible à destination de ———.
    G: Sie können dann Ihre Reise mit der nächsten Maschine nach ——— fortsetzen.
    I: Potrebbe continuare il viaggio con il primo volo per ———.
    P: Poderá continuar a sua viagem no próximo vôo disponível para ———.
    S: Ud. podría continuar el viaje en el primer vuelo que haya para ———.

89. **What about my luggage?**
    F: Et au sujet de mes bagages?
    G: Was wird mit meinem Gepäck geschehen?
    I: E il mio bagaglio?
    P: Que sucede à minha bagagem?
    S: ¿Qué pasará con mis valijas?

90. **We will send a telegram to our office at** ———.
    F: Nous allons envoyer un télégramme à notre bureau de ———.

* In Brazil *conosco*.

G: Wir werden unser Büro in ——— telegraphisch benachrichten.

I: Manderemo un telegramma al nostro ufficio di ———.

P: Enviaremos um telegrama para o nosso escritório em ———.

S: Mandaremos (OR Enviaremos) un telegrama a nuestra oficina en ———.

91. We will indicate in our message that ———.

F: Nous allons indiquer sur notre message que ———.

G: Wir werden veranlassen, daß ———.

I: Nel messaggio spiegheremo che ———.

P: Mencionaremos na nossa mensagem que ———.

S: Mencionaremos en nuestro mensaje que ———.

92. We will request them to locate your baggage at ———.

F: Nous allons leur demander de retrouver vos bagages à ———.

G: Wir werden veranlassen, daß Ihr Gepäck in ——— gefunden wird.

I: Richiederemo di rintracciare il Suo bagaglio a ———.

P: Pedir-lhe-emos que localizem a sua bagagem em ———.

S: Pediremos que localicen sus valijas en ———.

93. I would suggest your staying here in order to obtain your visa for ———.

F: Je vous suggère de rester ici de façon à obtenir votre visa pour ———.

G: Ich würde vorschlagen, daß Sie hier bleiben, um sich das Visum für ——— zu besorgen.

I: Le consiglio di rimanere qui in modo di ottenere il visto per ———.

P: Sugiro que fique aqui para obter o seu visto para ———.

S: Le recomiendo de quedarse aquí para poder obtener su visa para ———.

94. The Consulate might not be open over the weekend.

F: Le consulat peut être fermé pendant le weekend.

G: Das Konsulat ist vielleicht am Wochenende nicht geöffnet.

I: Il consolato potrebbe essere chiuso durante il fine-settimana.

P: O consulado não deve abrir durante o fim de semana.

S: El consulado no estará abierto durante el fin de semana.

Baggage and Seat Selection

F: BAGAGES ET CHOIX DES PLACES

G: GEPÄCK UND SITZWAHL

I: BAGAGLIO E RICHIESTA DEL POSTO

P: BAGAGEM E SELECÇÃO DE LUGARES

S: EQUIPAJE Y SELECCIÓN DE PLAZAS

95. May I have your ticket, please?

F: Puis-je avoir votre billet, s'il vous plaît?

G: Darf ich um Ihren Flugschein bitten?

I: Posso avere il Suo biglietto, per favore?

P: Faça favor o seu bilhete?

S: ¿Me permite su billete (OR boleto, pasaje)?

96. Do you have any hand baggage?

F: Avez-vous des bagages à main?

G: Haben Sie Handgepäck?

I: Ha del bagaglio a mano?

P: Tem alguma bagagem de mão?

S: ¿Tiene equipaje de mano?

97. I am sorry, but according to the regulations the following articles must be weighed:

F: Je suis désolé (FEM. désolée), mais d'après le règlement les articles suivants doivent être pesés:

G: Es tut mir leid, aber laut Vorschrift müssen folgende Gegenstände gewogen werden:

I: Mi dispiace, ma secondo il regolamento i seguenti oggetti devono essere pesati:

P: Tenho pena, mas de acordo com os regulamentos devem ser pesados os seguintes artigos:

S: Lo siento, pero de acuerdo con las normas se deben pesar los siguientes artículos:

98. Briefcases, portable typewriters.
F: Serviettes d'affaires, machines à écrire portatives.
G: Aktentaschen, Schreibmaschinen.
I: Borse, macchine da scrivere portabili.
P: Pastas, máquinas de escrever portáteis.
S: Carteras, máquinas de escribir portátiles.

99. Portable radios, vanity or cosmetic cases.
F: Postes de radio portatifs, sacs à main de dame.
G: Transistors, Kosmetikkoffer.
I: Radio portabili, necessaires o borsette da signora.
P: Rádios portáteis, malas de cosméticos.
S: Radios portátiles, neceseres.

100. Large camera cases.
F: Appareils photographiques ou cinématographiques de grandes dimensions.
G: Grosse Kameras.
I: Astucci con macchine fotografiche.
P: Câmaras fotográficas ou de filmar grandes.
S: Cámaras fotográficas grandes.

101. Hatboxes, overnight bags.
F: Cartons à chapeaux, petites valises de nuit.
G: Hutschachteln, Reisetaschen.
I: Cappelliere, borse.
P: Chapeleiras, sacos de mão (OR sacolas).
S: Sombrereras, bolsas de viaje.

102. Would you please put the camera on the scale?
F: Voulez-vous, s'il vous plaît, mettre l'appareil sur la balance?

G: Würden Sie bitte die Kamera auf die Waage legen?
I: Per favore, vuole mettere la macchina fotografica sulla bilancia?
P: Faça favor de pôr a câmara fotográfica na balança.
S: Por favor, ponga su cámara en la báscula (OR balanza).

103. I have to tag and weigh the baby carriage also.
F: Je dois étiqueter et peser la poussette du bébé aussi.
G: Der Kinderwagen muß auch gewogen und mit Gepäckanhänger versehen werden.
I: Devo pesare e mettere uno scontrino anche sulla carrozzina.
P: Tenho que etiquetar e pesar o carrinho do bébé também.
S: Debo rotular y pesar también el cochecito (OR cochecillo) de niños.

104. May I keep my baby carriage until boarding time?
F: Puis-je garder ma poussette jusqu'à l'embarquement?
G: Darf ich meinen Kinderwagen behalten, bis der Flug aufgerufen wird?
I: Posso tenere la carrozzina fino all'imbarco?
P: Posso conservar o carrinho do bébé até o momento de embarque?
S: ¿Podría usar el cochecito (OR cochecillo) hasta el momento de embarcar?

105. Yes, you may continue to use it, but only until boarding.
F: Oui, vous pouvez continuer à vous en servir jusqu'à l'embarquement.
G: Sie dürfen ihn behalten, aber nur bis zum Einsteigen.
I: Sì, può usarla fino al momento dell'imbarco.
P: Sim, pode continuar usá-lo até o embarque.
S: Sí, puede usarlo hasta el momento de embarcar.

106. Please do not forget to return the carriage to the same baggage counter as soon as your flight is announced.

F: S'il vous plaît, n'oubliez pas de rendre cette poussette au même comptoir dès que le départ de votre vol sera annoncé.

G: Vergessen Sie bitte nicht den Kinderwagen an dem selben Gepäckschalter abzugeben, sobald Ihr Flug aufgerufen ist.

I: Per favore, non dimentichi di riportare la carrozzina allo stesso banco dei bagagli appena il Suo volo sarà annunciato.

P: Por favor, não se esqueça de devolver o carrinho do bébé no mesmo balcão de bagagem logo que o seu vôo seja anunciado.

S: Por favor, no se olvide devolver el cochecito al mismo mostrador de equipaje en cuanto se anuncie su vuelo.

107. Do not go away! Stay here and wait for me!

F: Ne partez pas, restez ici et attendez-moi!

G: Gehen Sie nicht weg, bleiben Sie hier und warten Sie auf mich!

I: Non vada via, stia qui e mi aspetti!

P: Não se afaste, fique aqui e espere por mim.

S: Por favor, no se vaya, quédese aquí y espéreme.

108. Would you please put all your luggage on the scale?

F: Voulez-vous, s'il vous plaît, mettre tous vos bagages sur la bascule?

G: Würden Sie bitte Ihr gesamtes Gepäck auf die Waage legen?

I: Per favore, metta tutto il bagaglio sulla bilancia!

P: Por favor, coloque na balança toda a sua bagagem!

S: ¡Por favor, ponga todo su equipaje en la báscula (OR balanza)!

109. I am sorry, but we must hand-tag whatever you carry on board.

F: Je suis désolé (FEM. désolée), mais nous devons étiqueter tout ce que vous gardez à bord.

G: Es tut mir leid, aber wir müssen alle Stücke, die Sie mit an Bord nehmen, mit einem Anhänger versehen.

I: Mi dispiace, ma dobbiamo mettere uno scontrino a mano su tutto ciò che porta a bordo.

P: Tenho pena (OR Lamento), mas temos que etiquetar o que levar na cabina.

S: Lo siento, pero debemos rotular todo lo que lleve a bordo.

110. You have ——— pounds [kilos] of excess baggage.

F: Vous avez ——— livres [kilos] d'excédent de bagages.

G: Sie haben ——— Pfund [Kilo] Übergepäck.

I: Lei ha ——— libbre [chili] di eccedenza bagaglio.

P: Tem ——— libras [quilos] de excesso de bagagem.

S: Tiene ——— libras [kilos] de exceso de equipaje.

111. I do not understand. What do you mean by excess baggage?

F: Je ne comprends pas cela. Que voulez-vous dire par excédent de bagages?

G: Das verstehe ich nicht. Was meinen Sie mit Übergepäck?

I: Non capisco. Cosa vuole dire con eccedenza bagaglio?

P: Eu não compreendo isto. Que quer dizer por excesso de bagagem?

S: No lo comprendo. ¿Qué entiende Ud. por exceso de equipaje?

112. Please let me explain it to you!

F: Laissez-moi vous l'expliquer!

G: Ich will es Ihnen erklären!

I: Lasci che Le spieghi, prego!

P: Deixe-me explicar, por favor!

S: ¡Permítame explicarle!

113. The allowance according to the regulations is ——— pounds [kilos] for an Economy Class passenger.

F: D'après le règlement on admet en franchise ——— livres [kilos] en Classe Économique.

G: Laut Vorschriften dürfen Sie ——— Pfund [Kilo] für die Touristenklasse mitnehmen.

I: Secondo i regolamenti, il peso concesso è di ——— libbre [chili] per un passeggero in Classe Economica.

P: De acordo com os regulamentos o permitido é ——— libras [quilos] por cada passageiro de Classe Económica.

S: El peso permitido de acuerdo con las normas es ——— libras [kilos] para el pasajero de Clase Económica.

114. The allowance is ——— pounds [kilos] for a First Class passenger.

F: On admet ——— livres [kilos] en Première Classe.

G: Sie dürfen ——— Pfund [Kilo] für die Erste Klasse mitnehmen.

I: Il peso concesso è di ——— libbre [chili] per un passeggero in Prima Classe.

P: O permitido é ——— libras [quilos] por cada passageiro de Primeira Classe.

S: El peso permitido es ——— libras [kilos] para el pasajero de Primera Clase.

115. Please look at the scale now!

F: Regardez la bascule maintenant, s'il vous plaît!

G: Und jetzt sehen Sie bitte auf die Waage!

I: Ora, guardi la bilancia, prego!

P: Por favor, verifique a balança!

S: ¡Fíjese en la báscula (OR balanza), por favor!

116. You will see that the weight is ——— pounds [kilos].

F: Vous verrez que le poids est de ——— livres [kilos].

G: Sie werden feststellen, daß das Gewicht ——— Pfund [Kilo] beträgt.

I: Può vedere che il peso è di ——— libbre [chili].

P: Verificará que o peso é ——— libras [quilos].

S: Puede comprobar que el peso es ——— libras [kilos].

117. Listen! I have traveled a great deal, but my hand baggage has never been weighed before.

F: Écoutez! J'ai beaucoup voyagé mais mes bagages à main n'ont jamais encore été pesés.

G: Hören Sie mal zu! Ich bin schon sehr viel gereist, aber mein Handgepäck wurde niemals gewogen.

I: Senta, io ho viaggiato molto, ma il mio bagaglio a mano non è stato mai pesato.

P: Escute-me! Tenho viajado muitíssimo mas a minha bagagem de mão nunca foi pesada.

S: ¡Escuche! He viajado mucho pero mi equipaje nunca ha sido pesado.

118. I cannot possibly have an excess baggage weight.

F: Il est impossible que j'aie un excédent de bagages.

G: Es ist unmöglich, daß ich Übergepäck habe.

I: È impossibile! Non credo di avere eccedenza di peso.

P: É impossível que eu tenha excesso de peso.

S: Es imposible que yo tenga exceso de equipaje.

119. I have just come in from a flight on another airline.

F: Je viens d'arriver d'un vol avec une autre compagnie aérienne.

G: Ich bin gerade mit einer anderen Gesellschaft angekommen.

I: Sono appena arrivato con un volo di un'altra compagnia.

P: Acabo de chegar num vôo de outra companhia.

S: Acabo de llegar en un vuelo de otra compañía.

120. I was not charged for any excess weight.

F: On ne m'a pas chargé d'excédent de bagages.

G: Bei dieser Gesellschaft mußte ich nicht für Übergewicht bezahlen.

I: Non m'hanno fatto pagare eccedenza di peso.

P: Não me cobraram qualquer excesso de peso.

S: No tuve que pagar ningún gasto adicional por exceso de equipaje.

121. **It is possible that the agent who checked your baggage on the last occasion made an error.**

F: Il est possible que l'agent qui a enregistré vos bagages la dernière fois ait fait une erreur.

G: Es ist möglich, daß dem Angestellten, der Ihr Gepäck abgefertigt hat, bei dieser Gelegenheit ein Fehler unterlaufen ist.

I: Possibilmente il rappresentante che ha controllato il Suo bagaglio l'ultima volta ha fatto un errore.

P: É possível que o agente que processou a sua bagagem na última vez enganou-se.

S: Es posible que el empleado que comprobó su equipaje la última vez cometiera un error.

122. **I have not bought anything since I got off the other flight.**

F: Je n'ai rien acheté depuis que je suis descendu (FEM. descendue) de l'autre avion (OR appareil).

G: Seit meiner Ankunft mit der anderen Gesellschaft habe ich überhaupt nichts gekauft.

I: Non ho comprato niente da quando sono arrivato con l'altro aereo.

P: Eu não comprei mais nada desde que deixei o outro vôo.

S: No he comprado nada desde que salí del otro vuelo.

123. **Consequently, I cannot have any excess weight.**

F: En conséquence je ne peux pas avoir d'excédent.

G: Infolgedessen kann ich kein Übergepäck haben.

I: Perciò non posso avere eccedenza bagaglio.

P: Por tanto não posso ter qualquer excesso de peso.

S: Por lo tanto no puedo tener exceso de equipaje.

124. **Sir, I am very sorry, but I can only judge by the scale and the baggage you have for this flight.**

F: Je suis désolé (FEM. désolée), Monsieur, mais je ne puis que me référer à cette bascule et aux bagages que vous avez pour ce vol.

G: Ich bedauere es außerordentlich, aber ich kann mich nur nach der Waage und dem Gepäck, das Sie für diesen Flug haben, richten.

I: Signore, mi dispiace molto, ma io posso solo giudicare dalla bilancia e dal bagaglio che Lei ha per questo volo.

P: Lamento imenso, mas só posso ajuizar pela balança e pela bagagem que tem para este vôo.

S: Lo siento mucho, Señor, pero tengo que regirme por la báscula (OR balanza) y por el equipaje que lleva en este vuelo.

125. You have to pay ———.

F: Vous devez payer ———.

G: Sie haben ——— zu zahlen.

I: Lei deve pagare ———.

P: Tem que pagar ———.

S: Ud. debe pagar ———.

126. I would like to help you, but these are the rules.

F: Je voudrais vous aider mais c'est le règlement.

G: Ich würde Ihnen gerne helfen, aber so sind die Bestimmungen.

I: Vorrei poterLa aiutare ma questi sono i regolamenti.

P: Gostaria de ajudá-lo mas estes são os regulamentos.

S: Me agradaría poder ayudarle pero estas son las normas.

127. Excuse me. Now I have these other passengers to process.

F: Excusez-moi, maintenant je dois m'occuper de ces autres passagers.

G: Entschuldigen Sie mich jetzt bitte, ich habe noch alle diese Passagiere abzufertigen.

I: Scusi, ora devo occuparmi di questi altri passeggeri.

P: Desculpe-me, mas tenho agora que despachar estes outros passageiros.

S: Perdóneme (OR Discúlpeme, Dispénseme), debo atender ahora a estos otros pasajeros.

128. **I am sorry, but you may not take that bag as hand luggage.**
> F: Je suis désolé (FEM. désolée), mais vous ne pouvez pas garder ce bagage à bord.
> G: Es tut mir leid, aber Sie können diesen Koffer nicht als Handgepäck mitnehmen.
> I: Mi dispiace, ma Lei non può portare questa valigia a mano.
> P: Lamento, mas não pode levar essa mala como bagagem de mão.
> S: Lo siento, pero no puede llevar esa maleta como equipaje de mano.

129. **It is too big [too heavy].**
> F: Il est trop grand [trop lourd].
> G: Es ist zu groß [zu schwer].
> I: È troppo grande [troppo pesante].
> P: É muito grande [muito pesada].
> S: Es demasiado grande [demasiado pesada].

130. **The size, weight and amount of baggage carried by hand onto the airplane are limited by international regulations.**
> F: La taille, le poids et le nombre des bagages à main en cabine sont limités par des règlements internationaux.
> G: Die Größe, das Gewicht und die Anzahl der Gepäckstücke, die Sie als Handgepäck mit auf die Maschine nehmen dürfen, sind durch internationale Regeln festgesetzt.
> I: La grandezza, il peso, e il numero dei bagagli che si possono portare a mano a bordo è limitato da regolamenti internazionali.
> P: O tamanho, o peso e a quantidade de bagagem de mão na cabina está limitado por regulamentos internacionais.
> S: El tamaño, el peso y la cantidad de equipaje de mano que se puede llevar en el avión se limita por las normas internacionales.

131. In what part of the plane would you like to be seated?
- F: Où désirez-vous vous asseoir dans l'avion?
- G: In welchem Teil der Kabine möchten Sie sitzen?
- I: In quale parte dell'aereo vuole avere il Suo posto?
- P: Em que parte do avião gostaria de ter o seu lugar?
- S: ¿En qué parte del avión le gustaría sentarse?

132. I would like to be seated in the front [in the middle; in the rear].
- F: Je voudrais avoir mon siège en avant [au milieu; en arrière].
- G: Ich möchte vorn [in der Mitte; hinten] sitzen.
- I: Vorrei avere il mio posto avanti [in mezzo; dietro].
- P: Gostaria tê-lo na frente [no meio; na rectaguarda].
- S: Me gustaría sentarme en la parte delantera [en el medio; en la parte posterior] del avión.

133. I shall do my best to get a seat for you [beside the aisle].
- F: Je vais faire mon possible pour vous obtenir un siège [sur le couloir].
- G: Ich werde mein Möglichstes tun, Ihnen einen Sitz [am Gang] zu reservieren.
- I: Farò del mio meglio per ottenere un posto per Lei [accanto al corridoio].
- P: Farei o possível para arranjar-lhe um lugar [na coxia*].
- S: Haré quanto pueda por conseguirle un asiento [al lado del pasillo].

134. I prefer a seat in the center [over the wing; beside the window].
- F: Je préfère un siège au milieu [sur les ailes; à côté de la fenêtre (or à côté du hublot)].
- G: Ich bevorzuge einen Sitz in der Mitte [über der Tragfläche; am Fenster].

* In Brazil this would be *no corredor*.

I: Preferisco un posto al centro [sopra le ali; accanto al finestrino].

P: Prefiro um lugar ao meio [sobre a asa; perto da janela].

S: Prefiero un asiento en el medio [sobre las alas; al lado de la ventanilla].

135. Here is your ticket with the baggage checks for [Washington].

F: Voici votre billet avec vos reçus de bagage pour [Washington].

G: Hier ist Ihr Flugschein mit Ihrem Gepäckschein für [Washington].

I: Ecco il Suo biglietto con gli scontrini del bagaglio per [Washington].

P: Aqui tem o seu bilhete com as etiquetas de bagagem para [Washington].

S: Aquí tiene su billete (OR boleto, pasaje) con los comprobantes de su equipaje para [Washington].

136. The boarding of your flight, Number ———, is scheduled for ——— minutes past ——— o'clock at gate Number ———.

F: L'embarquement de votre vol, numéro ———, est prévu à ——— heures, ——— minutes, porte numéro ———.

G: Wir rufen den Flug Nummer ——— um ——— Uhr und ——— Minuten auf, Ausgang Nummer ———.

I: L'imbarco del Suo volo, numero ———, è previsto per le ——— ore e minuti——— all'uscita numero———.

P: O embarque de seu vôo, número ———, está marcado para ——— horas, ——— minutos, pela porta número ———.

S: De acuerdo con el plan de vuelo, su embarque se efectuará a las ——— horas, ——— minutos, por la puerta número ———.

137. On boarding, please present this envelope.

F: En embarquant présentez, s'il vous plaît, cette enveloppe.

G: Beim Einsteigen zeigen Sie bitte diesen Umschlag.
I: All'imbarco, per favore, mostri questa busta.
P: Ao embarque mostre este envelope, por favor.
S: Presente este sobre al embarcar, por favor.

138. Goodbye. Thank you. Have a nice trip!
   F: Au revoir. Merci beaucoup. Je vous souhaite un bon voyage!
   G: Vielen Dank und auf Wiedersehen! Wir wünschen Ihnen einen angenehmen Flug!
   I: ArrivederLa. Grazie. Buon viaggio!
   P: Adeus. Obrigado (FEM. Obrigada). Boa viagem!
   S: Adiós. Muchas gracias. ¡Buen viaje!

Before Boarding (In the Passenger Lounge)

   F: AVANT L'EMBARQUEMENT (*Dans la salle d'attente*)
   G: VOR DEM EINSTEIGEN (*Im Warteraum*)
   I: PRIMA DELL'IMBARCO (*Nella sala d'aspetto*)
   P: ANTES DO EMBARQUE (*Na sala de espera*)
   S: ANTES DE EMBARCAR (*En la sala de espera*)

139. Are you one of our passengers on Flight Number ——— to ———?
   F: Êtes-vous un de nos passagers du vol numéro ——— pour ———?
   G: Sind Sie Passagier für Flug Nummer ——— nach ———?
   I: Lei è in partenza con il volo numero ——— per ———?
   P: É o senhor nosso passageiro (TO FEM. É a senhora nossa passageira) no vôo número ——— para ———?
   S: ¿Es Ud. pasajero del vuelo número ——— para ———?

140. *To the children:* **Are you going to fly with us today?**
F: *Aux enfants:* Allez-vous voler avec nous aujourd'hui?
G: *Zu den Kindern:* Fliegt ihr heute mit uns?
I: *Ai bambini:* Volate con noi oggi?
P: *Aos meninos:* Vôam connosco* hoje?
S: *A los niños:* ¿Vais a volar con nosotros hoy?

141. *To a mother:* **Let me assist you!**
F: *À une mère:* Laissez-moi vous aider!
G: *Zu einer Mutter:* Darf ich Ihnen behilflich sein?
I: *A una madre:* L'aiuto io?
P: *A uma mãe:* Deixe-me ajudá-la!
S: *A una madre:* ¡Permítame ayudarle!

142. Do you mind waiting for a moment?
F: Verriez-vous un inconvénient à attendre un instant?
G: Darf ich Sie bitten, einen Augenblick zu warten?
I: Le dispiace di aspettare un momento?
P: Não se importa de esperar um momento?
S: Por favor, espere un momento.

143. I will contact the ground personnel; they will answer your question.
F: Je vais contacter le personnel au sol; ils répondront à votre question.
G: Ich werde mich mit dem Bodenpersonal in Verbindung setzen. Das Bodenpersonal wird Ihre Frage beantworten können.
I: Chiamerò il personale di terra che risponderà alle Sue domande.
P: Vou chamar o pessoal de terra† para responder à sua pergunta.
S: Hablaré con el personal de tierra que contestará a su pregunta.

---

* In Brazil *conosco.*
† In Brazil *os funcionarios de terra.*

144. Please stay here until your flight is announced.
F: Veuillez, s'il vous plaît, rester ici jusqu'à l'appel de votre vol.
G: Ritte, bleiben Sie hier, bis Ihr Flug ausgerufen wird.
I: Per favore, stia qui fino all'annuncio del Suo volo.
P: Por favor, fique aqui até o seu vôo ser anunciado.
S: Por favor, quédese aquí hasta que anuncien el vuelo.

145. Your flight has not yet been announced.
F: Votre vol n'a pas encore été annoncé.
G: Bis jetzt ist Ihr Flug noch nicht ausgerufen.
I: Il Suo volo non è stato ancora annunciato.
P: O seu vôo não foi ainda anunciado.
S: Su vuelo no ha sido anunciado todavía.

146. Your flight is ——— hours [minutes] late.
F: Votre vol est en retard de ——— heures [minutes].
G: Ihr Flug hat ——— Stunden [Minuten] Verspätung.
I: Il Suo volo è ——— ore [minuti] in ritardo.
P: O seu vôo está atrazado ——— horas [minutos].
S: Su vuelo lleva ——— horas [minutos] de retraso (OR atraso).

147. Tell me, please, at which gate do I have to board the plane?
F: Dites-moi, s'il vous plaît, quelle est la porte d'embarquement?
G: Sagen Sie mir bitte, durch welchen Ausgang komme ich zu meinem Flugzeug?
I: Mi dice, per favore, da quale uscita si va a bordo?
P: Diga-me, por favor, qual é a porta por que devo embarcar?
S: Dígame, por favor, ¿por cuál puerta debo salir para embarcar?

148. At Gate Number ———.
F: Par la porte numéro ———.
G: Zum Ausgang Nummer ———.

I: Dall'uscita numero ———.
P: Pela porta número ———.
S: Por la puerta número ———.

149. May I see your boarding card?
   F: Puis-je voir votre carte d'embarquement?
   G: Darf ich um Ihre Bordkarte bitten?
   I: Posso vedere la Sua carta d'imbarco?
   P: Posso ver o seu cartão de embarque?
   S: ¿Puedo ver su tarjeta de embarque?

150. Do not forget that your flight leaves from Gate Number ———.
   F: N'oubliez pas que votre vol part de la porte numéro ———.
   G: Bitte vergessen Sie nicht, daß Ihr Flug am Ausgang Nummer ——— aufgerufen wird.
   I: Non dimentichi che il Suo volo parte dall'uscita numero ———.
   P: Favor não esquecer que o seu vôo parte da porta número ———.
   S: No se olvide de que debe embarcar por la puerta número ———.

151. Do you serve a meal immediately after take-off?
   F: Servez-vous le repas immédiatement après le décollage?
   G: Gibt es gleich nach dem Start etwas zu essen?
   I: Il pranzo sarà servito subito dopo il decollo?
   P: Servem uma refeição imediatamente após a partida?
   S: ¿Sirven comidas inmediatamente después del despegue?

152. There is a meal service scheduled about an hour after take-off.
   F: Il y a un repas prévu pour une heure environ après le décollage.
   G: Ungefähr eine Stunde nach dem Start wird das Essen serviert.

I: Il pranzo sarà servito a un'ora circa dopo il decollo.
P: Há uma refeição marcada cerca de uma hora após a partida.
S: Se sirve una comida alrededor de una hora después del despegue.

153. Is there liquor available on this flight?
F: Peut-on obtenir des liqueurs sur ce vol?
G: Gibt es alkoholische Getränke auf dem Flug?
I: Servono liquori a bordo?
P: Haverá bebidas neste vôo?
S: ¿Se sirven bebidas en este vuelo?

154. There are complimentary drinks in First Class.
F: Les liqueurs sont gratuites en Première Classe.
G: In der Ersten Klasse sind die Getränke frei.
I: Saranno offerti liquori in Prima Classe.
P: Há bebidas gratuitas na Primeira Classe.
S: Se sirven bebidas gratuitas en Primera Clase.

155. In the Economy Section drinks are available at a nominal charge.
F: En Classe Économique on peut obtenir les liqueurs au prix coûtant.
G: In der Touristenklasse können Sie für wenig Geld Getränke erhalten.
I: In Classe Economica i liquori sono in vendita al prezzo di costo.
P: Na Classe Económica há bebidas a venda a um custo nominal.
S: En Clase Económica se venden bebidas a precio de costo.

156. Are the flights rough at the altitudes at which you fly?
F: Les vols sont-ils mouvementés à l'altitude où vous volez?
G: Ist der Flug sehr unruhig in der Höhe, in der Sie fliegen?

I: È scomodo il volo all'altezza che volate?
P: É inconfortável às altitudes que vôam?
S: ¿Es molesto viajar a la altura que vuelan?

157. According to the captain we expect a smooth flight this evening.

F: D'après le capitaine nous aurons un vol tranquille ce soir.
G: Nach der Ansicht unseres Kapitäns werden wir heute abend einen sehr ruhigen Flug haben.
I: Il Capitano ci informa che questa sera avremo un volo tranquillo.
P: De acordo com o capitão esperamos um vôo suave (OR calmo) esta noite.
S: Según el capitán (OR comandante) esperamos un vuelo tranquilo para esta tarde.

158. What is the cruising altitude?

F: Quelle est l'altitude de croisière?
G: In welcher Höhe fliegen Sie?
I: Qual'è l'altezza di crociera?
P: Qual é a altitude de cruzeiro?
S: ¿Cuál es la altura de crucero?

159. About ——— feet, approximately ——— meters.

F: Environ ——— pieds, approximativement ——— mètres.
G: In ungefähr ——— Fuß, um ——— Meter.
I: Circa ——— piedi, cioè circa ——— metri.
P: Cerca de ——— pés, aproximadamente ——— metros.
S: Alrededor de ——— pies, es decir unos ——— metros.

160. I was promised a bassinet. Do you think it will be available?

F: On m'avait promis une bassinette (OR un berceau). Pensez-vous qu'elle (OR il) sera disponible?

G: Mir wurde ein Babybettchen versprochen. Glauben Sie, daß ich es bekommen kann?

I: Mi hanno promesso una culla. Crede che potrò averla?

P: Prometeram-me um berço. Pensa que haverá?

S: Me prometieron una cunita. ¿Cree Ud. que me la facilitarán?

161. May I see your ticket (with the envelope)?

F: Puis-je voir votre billet (avec l'enveloppe)?

G: Darf ich bitte Ihren Flugschein (mit dem Kuvert— OR Umschlag) sehen?

I: Posso vedere il Suo biglietto (con la busta)?

P: Posso ver o seu bilhete (com o envelope)?

S: ¿Puedo ver su pasaje (con el sobre)?

162. Your seat is facing the bulkhead, where the bassinet will be located.

F: Votre siège est au premier rang, où sera la bassinette (OR le berceau).

G: Ihr Sitz befindet sich direkt hinter der Trennwand. Dort ist das Babybettchen.

I: Il Suo posto è di fronte alla partizione, dove sarà posta la culla.

P: O seu lugar é ao pé da divisão, onde o berço será colocado.

S: Su asiento queda en frente de la separación, donde irá colocada la cunita.

163. I will check with the purser to see if we can put you in a three-seat row.

F: Je vais vérifier avec le commissaire de bord si nous pouvons vous donner trois sièges sur le même rang.

G: Ich werde mich mit dem Chefsteward in Verbindung setzen und versuchen, für Sie drei Sitze nebeneinander zu bekommen.

I: Controllerò con il commissario di bordo se possiamo farLa sedere in una fila di tre posti.

P: Verificarei com o comissário se poderemos dar-lhe uma fila de três lugares.

S: Voy a consultar con el comisario de abordo si pueden ocupar una fila de tres asientos.

164. I will remove the arm rests and then I will make a little bassinet for the child.

F: Je vais enlever les accoudoirs et puis je vais préparer un petit berceau pour l'enfant.

G: Ich werde die Armlehnen herausnehmen und dann werde ich ein Bettchen für das Kind machen.

I: Toglierò i braccioli e poi farò una piccola culla per il bambino.

P: Retirarei os apoios dos braços e em seguida prepararei um berço para a criança.

S: Quitaré los brazos de los asientos y luego prepararé una cunita para el niño.

165. *To an aged or incapacitated passenger in a wheelchair or to a mother with children:* **Please remain calm. When your flight is announced I will come back to assist you aboard myself.**

F: *À un passager âgé ou infirme dans une chaise roulante ou à une mère avec enfants:* S'il vous plaît, restez tranquille. Quand votre vol sera annoncé je viendrai moi-même vous aider à embarquer.

G: *Zu einem älteren oder behinderten Passagier mit Rollstuhl oder zu einer Mutter mit Kindern:* Bitte bleiben Sie ruhig. Wenn Ihr Flug ausgerufen wird, werde ich selber Sie abholen und in die Maschine bringen.

I: *A un passeggero anziano o a un invalido sulla sedia a rotelle o a una madre con bambini:* Prego di rimanere tranquillo (TO FEM. tranquilla). Io ritornerò quando sarà chiamato il Suo volo per assisterLa all'imbarco.

P: *A um passageiro* (FEM. *uma passageira*) *de idade o
incapacitado* (FEM. *incapacitada*) *em cadeira de rodas
ou a uma mãe com crianças:* Por favor, conserve-se
tranquilo (TO FEM. tranquila). Quando o seu vôo for
anunciado voltarei para assistir o seu embarque.

S: *A un pasajero de edad avanzada o incapacitado en
silla de ruedas o a una madre con niños:* Por favor,
permanezca tranquilo (TO FEM. tranquila). Cuando
su vuelo se anuncie volveré para acompañarle abordo.

166. When do we take off?
F: Quand décollons-nous?
G: Wann fliegen wir ab?
I: Quando decolliamo?
P: Quando descolamos?*
S: ¿Cuándo despegamos?

167. As soon as everything is perfectly all right.
F: Dès que tout sera en ordre.
G: Sobald alles in Ordnung ist.
I: Appena tutto sarà pronto.
P: Tão cedo tudo esteja pronto.
S: Tan pronto como todo esté en regla (OR en orden).

168. What is the reason for the delay?
F: Quelle est la raison du délai?
G: Was ist der Grund für die Verspätung?
I: Qual'è la ragione del ritardo?
P: Qual é a razão para o atrazo?
S: ¿Cuál es el motivo del retraso (OR del atraso, de la
demora)?

169. The air traffic is unusually heavy this evening.
F: Le trafic aérien est anormalement intense ce soir.
G: Wir haben ungewöhnlich starken Flugverkehr heute
abend.

* In Brazil *decolamos*.

I: Questa sera il traffico aereo è particolarmente intenso.
P: O tráfego aéreo é muito intenso esta noite.
S: El tráfico aéreo es demasiado intenso esta tarde.

170. **We have to wait until the storm is over [until the rain stops; until the fog lifts].**
F: Nous devons attendre jusqu'à ce que l'orage soit fini [jusqu'à ce que la pluie s'arrête; jusqu'à ce que le brouillard se dissipe].
G: Wir müssen warten bis sich der Sturm gelegt hat [bis der Regen aufgehört hat; bis der Nebel sich gehoben hat].
I: Si deve aspettare finchè cessi il temporale [finchè cessi la pioggia; finchè la nebbia si diradi].
P: Temos que esperar que a tempestade pare [que a chuva pare; que o nevoeiro levante].
S: Tendremos que esperar hasta que la tormenta pare [hasta que la lluvia pare; hasta que se levante la niebla*].

171. **We are waiting for an improvement in weather conditions.**
F: Nous attendons une amélioration des conditions météorologiques.
G: Wir warten auf Wetterbesserung.
I: Si aspetta un miglioramento delle condizioni atmosferiche.
P: Estamos a espera duma melhoria das condições atmosféricas.
S: Esperamos que el tiempo mejore.

172. **Can I send a telegram?**
F: Puis-je envoyer un télégramne?
G: Besteht die Möglichkeit, ein Telegramm abzuschicken?
I: Posso mandare (OR spedire) un telegramma?
P: Posso enviar um telegrama?
S: ¿Puedo enviar un telegrama?

* *La neblina* in South America.

173. Here is a telegram form for you.
F: Voici un formulaire de télégramme pour vous.
G: Hier haben Sie ein Telegrammformular.
I: Ecco un modulo per telegramma.
P: Aqui tem um impresso de telegrama.
S: Aqui tiene un formulario (OR impreso) de telegrama.

174. I want to change my hotel reservation.
F: Je veux changer ma réservation d'hôtel.
G: Ich möchte meine Buchung für das Hotel ändern.
I: Vorrei cambiare la mia prenotazione d'albergo.
P: Quero alterar a minha reserva de hotel.
S: Deseo cambiar la reservación (OR reserva) de mi hotel.

175. Am I going to miss my connecting flight?
F: Est-ce que je vais manquer ma correspondance?
G: Werde ich meinen Anschlußflug verpassen?
I: Perderò la coincidenza (OR il mio volo in coincidenza)?
P: Perderei o meu vôo em ligação?
S: ¿Voy a perder mi vuelo de conexión?

176. I do not think so.
F: Je ne le pense pas.
G: Ich glaube nicht.
I: Non credo.
P: Penso que não.
S: No lo creo.

Boarding; Flight; Arrival

F: EMBARQUEMENT; VOL; ARRIVÉE
G: EINSTEIGEN; FLUG; ANKUNFT
I: IMBARCO; VOLO; ARRIVO
P: EMBARQUE; VÔO; CHEGADA
S: EMBARQUE; VUELO; LLEGADA

Seating of Passengers

F: EMPLACEMENT DES PASSAGERS
G: SETZEN DER PASSAGIERE
I: ACCOMODAMENTO DEI PASSEGGERI
P: ACOMODAÇÃO DOS PASSAGEIROS
S: ACOMODACIÓN DE LOS PASAJEROS

177. May I see your ticket?
F: Puis-je voir votre billet?
G: Darf ich um Ihren Flugschein bitten?
I: Posso vedere il Suo biglietto?
P: Posso ver o seu bilhete?
S: ¿Puedo ver su billete (OR boleto, pasaje)?

178. Your seat is behind the partition.
F: Votre siège est derrière la partition.
G: Ihr Sitz is hinter der Trennwand.
I: Il Suo posto è dietro la partizione.
P: O seu lugar (OR assento) è atrás da divisão.
S: Su asiento está situado trás la separación.

179. Walk straight ahead and to the rear.
F: Dirigez-vous tout droit vers l'arrière de l'appareil.
G: Gehen Sie bitte geradeaus in den hinteren Teil der Kabine.
I: Vada diritto in fondo.
P: Dirija-se para a rectaguarda.
S: Camine adelante dirigiéndose hacia el fondo.

180. The stewardess there will show you where your seat is.

F: L'hôtesse là-bas vous indiquera votre siège.

G: Dort wird Ihnen die Stewardeß Ihren Sitz zeigen.

I: La hostess Le farà vedere lì il Suo posto.

P: A hospedeira* lá indicar-lhe-á onde é o seu lugar.

S: La stewardess† ahí le indicará su asiento.

181. Would you mind proceeding to the rear [to the front], where your seat is located?

F: Voulez-vous, s'il vous plaît, vous diriger vers l'arrière [vers l'avant], où se trouve votre siège?

G: Würden Sie sich bitte nach hinten [nach vorne] bemühen, wo sich Ihr Sitz befindet?

I: Le dispiace proseguire verso il fondo [davanti], dove si trova il Suo posto?

P: Por favor, dirija-se para a rectaguarda [para a frente], onde é o seu lugar.

S: Por favor, diríjase hacia el fondo [al frente], donde se halla su asiento.

182. You have Seat Number ——— right here [beside the aisle; in the center].

F: Vous avez le siège numéro ——— juste ici [sur le couloir; au milieu].

G: Ihr Sitz ist Nummer ———, gerade hier [am Gang; in der Mitte].

I: Il Suo posto è numero ——— proprio qui [accanto al corridoio; al centro].

P: Tem o lugar número ———, aqui mesmo [na coxia;‡ ao meio].

S: Ud. tiene el asiento número ——— justo aquí [al lado del pasillo; en el centro].

---

* In Brazil *aeromoça*.

† Also; in Spain *azafata*; in South America *aeromoza, cabinera, auxiliar* (OR *asistente*) *de vuelo*.

‡ In Brazil *no corredor*.

183. **Your seat is beside the window [——— rows to the rear; ——— rows ahead].**

   F: Votre siège est à côté de la fenêtre [——— rangs à l'arrière; ——— rangs à l'avant].

   G: Ihr Sitz ist am Fenster [——— Reihen nach hinten; ——— Reihen nach vorne].

   I: Il Suo posto è accanto al finestrino [——— file dietro; ——— file avanti].

   P: O seu lugar é à janela [——— filas para a rectaguarda; ——— filas para a frente].

   S: Su asiento está al lado de la ventanilla [——— filas hacia atrás; ——— filas hacia delante].

184. **We were told we would be seated all together!**

   F: On nous avait dit que nous serions assis tous (FEM. assises toutes) ensemble!

   G: Uns wurde versprochen, daß wir zusammen sitzen können!

   I: Ci hanno detto che avremmo avuto i posti vicini!

   P: Disseram-nos que ficávamos sentados juntos (FEM. sentadas juntas)!

   S: Nos dijeron que estaríamos sentados todos juntos (FEM. sentadas todas juntas).

185. **What can you do about it?**

   F: Que pouvez-vous faire pour arranger cela?

   G: Können Sie da etwas tun?

   I: Come ci può sistemare (OR accomodare)?

   P: O que é que pode fazer?

   S: ¿Qué puede hacer acerca de esto?

186. **Would you please take the seat assigned to you for the time being?**

   F: Pouvez-vous, s'il vous plaît, garder pour le moment le siège qui vous à été donné (OR assigné)?

   G: Bitte behalten Sie im Augenblick noch den Platz, der Ihnen zugewiesen wurde.

I: Per il momento voglia accomodarsi al posto che Le
hanno assegnato.
P: Se não se importa, use temporàriamente o assento que
lhe foi marcado.
S: ¿Quiere tomar por ahora el asiento que le ha sido
asignado?

187. I am very sorry that this happened.
F: Je suis désolé (FEM. désolée) que ceci soit arrivé.
G: Ich bedauere sehr, daß so etwas passierte.
I: Sono spiacente dell'accaduto.
P: Lamento imenso que isto tivesse acontecido.
S: Siento lo sucedido.

188. After the take-off I will come back.
F: Je reviendrai après le décollage.
G: Nach dem Start werde ich zu Ihnen kommen.
I: Dopo il decollo tornerò.
P: Após a descolagem eu voltarei.
S: Después de despegar volveré.

189. I will do my best to seat you together.
F: Je vais faire mon possible pour vous asseoir ensemble.
G: Ich werde mein Möglichstes tun, um Sie zusammen zu
setzen.
I: Farò il possibile per farVi sedere vicino (OR insieme).
P: Farei o possível para sentá-los juntos (TO FEM. sentá-
las juntas).
S: Haré todo lo que pueda para acomodarles juntos (TO
FEM. juntas).

**190. I will see if those passengers would not mind moving
to other seats.**
F: Je vais demander si ces passagers-là ne voient pas
d'inconvénient à changer de sièges.
G: Vielleicht haben diese Passagiere nichts dagegen,
andere Plätze einzunehmen.

I: Vedrò se a questi passeggeri non dispiace spostarsi ad un altro posto.
P: Vou ver se aqueles passageiros não se importam de mudar de lugares.
S: Veré si a esos pasajeros no les importa cambiar de asientos.

191. Would you be so kind as to move to your seat, Number ———? It's over there on the left.
F: Ayez l'obligeance d'aller occuper votre siège, numéro ———. C'est là-bas, à gauche.
G: Wären Sie bitte so freundlich und würden Sie sich zu Ihrem Platz, Nummer ———, begeben? Er ist dort drüben, links.
I: Le spiacerebbe sedersi al Suo posto, numero ———, là sulla sinistra?
P: Tenha a amabilidade de ir para o seu lugar, número ———, que é ali à esquerda.
S: ¿Tendría la bondad de ocupar su asiento, número ———? Está ahí, a la izquierda.

192. This seat is occupied, but that one on the right is free.
F: Ce siège est occupé, mais celui-là à droite est libre.
G: Dieser Sitz ist besetzt, aber der auf der rechten Seite ist frei.
I: Questo posto è occupato ma quello sulla destra è libero.
P: Este lugar está ocupado mas aquele à direita está livre.
S: Este asiento está ocupado pero el a la derecha está libre.

193. I was promised a seat over the wing.
F: On m'avait promis un siège sur les ailes.
G: Mir wurde ein Sitz über den Flügeln versprochen.
I: Mi avevano promesso un posto sopra le ali.
P: Prometeram-me um lugar sobre a asa.
S: Me prometieron un asiento sobre las alas.

194. When I made my reservation I requested a special seat.

F: Quand j'ai fait ma réservation, j'ai demandé un siège déterminé.

G: Als ich meine Buchung machte, bat ich um einen besonderen Sitz.

I: Quando ho fatto la prenotazione ho richiesto un posto particolare.

P: Quando fiz a minha reserva pedi um lugar especial.

S: Cuando hice mi reservación pedí un asiento (OR una plaza) especial.

195. I will check on this right away. Excuse me!

F: Je vais vérifier cela immédiatement. Excusez-moi!

G: Ich werde es sofort überprüfen. Entschuldigen Sie mich bitte!

I: Vado a controllare subito. Mi scusi!

P: Vou verificar imediatamente. Desculpe-me!

S: Lo comprobaré (OR verificaré) inmediatamente. ¡Discúlpeme!

196. I am very sorry, Sir, but we have no record of your request.

F: Je suis désolé (FEM. désolée), Monsieur, mais nous n'avons pas trace de votre demande.

G: Es tut mir außerordentlich leid, aber wir haben keine Unterlagen über Ihre Platzbestellung.

I: Sono spiacente, Signore, ma la Sua richiesta non è stata segnalata.

P: Lamento sinceramente, mas não temos registo do seu pedido.

S: Lo lamento, Señor, pero no tenemos nota de su petición (OR pedido).

197. However, I will try to make some arrangement to obtain that seat for you.

F: Néanmoins je vais essayer de vous obtenir ce siège.

G: Trotzdem werde ich mein Möglichstes tun, damit Sie diesen Platz behalten.

I: In ogni modo farò del mio meglio per ottenere il posto che Lei desidera.

P: Contudo tentarei fazer por obter aquele lugar para si.

S: Sin embargo haré todo lo posible para conseguirle ese asiento.

198. I can understand your disappointment.

F: Je comprends votre mécontentement.

G: Selbstverständlich verstehe ich Ihre Unzufriedenheit.

I: Capisco il disappunto.

P: Compreendo o seu desapontamento.

S: Comprendo perfectamente su contrariedad.

199. I assume there was a misunderstanding.

F: Je suppose qu'il y ait eu un malentendu.

G: Ich nehme an, daß es sich um ein Mißverständnis handelt.

I: Presumo ci sia stato un errore.

P: Suponho que houve um malentendido.

S: Supongo que hubo un malentendido (or malentendimiento).

200. We have a center seat available as an alternate.

F: Nous avons disponible comme alternative un siège au milieu.

G: Statt dessen könnten wir Ihnen einen Mittelsitz anbieten.

I: Saremo felici di offrirLe invece un posto di centro che è libero.

P: Como alternativa temos um lugar disponível no centro.

S: Podemos ofrecerle un asiento en el medio como alternativa.

201. We would be happy to let you sit there.

F: Nous serions heureux que vous l'occupiez.

G: Es würde uns freuen, wenn Sie diesen Sitz annehmen würden.

I: Saremmo felici se volesse accomodarsi lì.
P: Ficaremos contentes se quer ocupá-lo.
S: Nos agradará que lo ocupe.

202. We are sorry, but we have to request you to return to your original seat at the next stop.

F: Nous regrettons, mais vous devrez reprendre votre propre siège à la prochaine escale.

G: Es tut uns leid, aber wir müssen Sie bitten, bei der nächsten Zwischenlandung Ihren ursprünglichen Sitz wieder einzunehmen.

I: Ci dispiace, ma a un prossimo scalo La preghiamo di ritornare al posto originalmente assegnatoLe.

P: Lamento, mas devemos pedi-lhe que regresse ao seu lugar original na próxima paragem (OR estação, escala).

S: Lo siento, pero le debemos rogar que vuelva a su asiento original en la próxima escala.

203. I would like to have your name and address and the approximate date and place of your reservation.

F: Voulez-vous, s'il vous plaît, me donner votre nom et votre adresse, ainsi que la date approximative et le lieu de votre réservation?

G: Darf ich Sie um Ihren Namen und Ihre Adresse, sowie um das ungefähre Datum und den Ort Ihrer Reservierung (OR Buchung) bitten?

I: Vorrei avere il Suo nome e indirizzo, e approssimativamente la data e luogo della Sua prenotazione.

P: Gostaríamos de ter o seu nome e endereço (OR morada) e a data aproximada e o local da sua reserva.

S: Déme su nombre y dirección por favor, y también la fecha aproximada y el lugar de su reservación.

204. We shall report this discrepancy to our superiors.

F: Nous allons rapporter cet incident à nos supérieurs.

G: Wir werden dieses Vorkommnis unserer zuständigen Stelle melden.

I: Riporteremo questo inconveniente alla nostra direzione.

P: Informaremos os nossos superiores desta irregularidade.

S: Informaremos de este incidente a nuestros superiores.

205. **I will try to reserve an aisle seat for you on our departure from ———.**

F: Je vais essayer de vous réserver un siège-couloir quand nous partirons de ———.

G: Ich werde versuchen, Ihnen einen Sitz am Gang zu reservieren, wenn wir von ——— abfliegen.

I: Alla partenza da ——— cercherò di riservarLe un posto di corridoio.

P: Tentarei reservar-lhe um lugar de coxia* quando partiremos de ———.

S: Intentaré reservarle un asiento junto al pasillo cuando partamos de ———.

206. **Perhaps at another stop there will be a window seat available.**

F: Il y aura peut-être un siège-fenêtre disponible à une autre escale.

G: Vielleicht wird ein Fenstersitz bei einer anderen Zwischenlandung frei.

I: Potrebbe darsi che ad un altro scalo ci sia un posto al finestrino libero.

P: Talvez noutra estação exista um lugar de janela vago.

S: Quizás en otra escala haya un asiento de ventanilla vacante.

207. **Is it possible to get more fresh air?**

F: Est-il possible d'obtenir plus d'air frais?

G: Ist es möglich, etwas mehr frische Luft zu bekommen?

I: È possibile avere più aria?

P: É possível aumentar o ar fresco?

S: ¿Podríamos tener más aire fresco?

* In Brazil *de corredor*.

208. I am sorry, the air conditioning does not work until we are aloft.

F: Je suis désolé (FEM. désolée), mais le système d'air conditionné ne fonctionne qu'en vol.

G: Es tut mir leid, aber das Luftkühlungssystem funktioniert erst nach dem Start.

I: Sono spiacente, ma l'aria condizionata non funziona mentre non siamo in volo.

P: Tenho pena, mas o ar condicionado não trabalha emquanto não subirmos.

S: Lo siento, el aire acondicionado no funciona hasta que estemos en vuelo.

209. Would you like a wet towel and a cold drink?

F: Désirez-vous une serviette humide et des rafraîchissements?

G: Möchten Sie ein feuchtes Tuch und Erfrischungsgetränke haben?

I: Desidera avere una salvietta umida per rinfrescarsi e qualcosa di fresco da bere?

P: Gostaria de ter uma toalha húmida e uma bebida fresca?

S: ¿Quiere una toalla húmeda y alguna bebida fresca?

210. Tell me, please, has all my luggage been loaded on the airplane?

F: Dites-moi, s'il vous plaît, mes bagages ont-ils bien été mis à bord?

G: Bitte sagen Sie mir, ob mein ganzes Gepäck ins Flugzeug verladen ist.

I: Mi dica, per favore, se tutti i miei bagagli sono stati messi (OR caricati) a bordo.

P: Diga-me, por favor, foi toda a minha bagagem carregada no avião?

S: Dígame, por favor, si han cargado todo mi equipaje en el avión.

211. Let me install the bassinet for your baby.
F: Laissez-moi installer le berceau (OR la bassinette) pour votre bébé.
G: Gestatten Sie, daß ich das Bettchen für Ihr Baby installiere.
I: Mi permetta di mettere la culla per il Suo bebe.
P: Deixe-me instalar o berço para o seu bébé.
S: Permítame instalarle la cunita para el niño.

212. Is this bassinet safe on take-off, on landing and during turbulence?
F: Ce berceau est-il sûr (OR en sécurité) pendant le décollage, pendant l'atterrissage et en cas de mauvais temps?
G: Ist das Bettchen sicher genug beim Start, beim Landen und bei unruhigem Wetter?
I: La culla è stabile durante il decollo, durante l'atterraggio e con delle turbulenze (OR con dei vuoti d'aria)?
P: É este berço de segurança na descolagem, na aterragem e durante a turbulência?
S: ¿Va segura la cunita durante el despegue, al aterrizar y durante tiempo tormentoso?

213. Would you please put your handbag [your camera (*if it is big*)] underneath your seat?
F: Voulez-vous, s'il vous plaît, mettre votre sac à main [votre appareil photographique (*si c'est grand*)] sous votre siège?
G: Würden Sie bitte Ihre Handtasche [Ihren Photo-apparat (*falls er groß ist*)] unter Ihren Sitz legen?
I: La prego di mettere la Sua borsa [la macchina foto-grafica (*se è grande*)] sotto il Suo sedile.
P: Poderia pôr a sua mala de mão [a sua câmara (*se é grande*)] por baixo do seu assento?
S: ¿Quiere poner por favor su bolsa [su cámara (*si es grande*)] bajo su asiento?

214. Please put your camera (*if it is small*) into the seat pocket.

F: Mettez, s'il vous plaît, votre appareil photographique (*si c'est petit*) dans la pochette du fauteuil.

G: Stecken Sie bitte Ihre Kamera (*falls sie klein ist*) in die Sitztasche.

I: La prego di mettere la macchina fotografica (*se è piccola*) nella tasca del sedile.

P: Por favor, ponha a sua câmara (*se é pequena*) na bolsa da cadeira.

S: Ponga por favor su cámara (*si es pequeña*) en el bolsillo del asiento.

215. I am sorry, but you must not put any heavy object on the hat rack that might fall on the heads of the passengers in case of turbulence.

F: Je suis désolé (FEM. désolée), mais vous ne devez mettre dans le filet aucun objet lourd pouvant tomber sur la tête des passagers en cas de mauvais temps.

G: Es tut mir leid, aber Sie dürfen keine schweren Gegenstände in das Gepäcknetz legen. Sie könnten bei unruhigem Wetter den Passagieren auf den Kopf fallen!

I: Sono spiacente, ma non si può mettere nessun oggetto pesante sopra la rete (OR reticella). Potrebbe cadere sulla testa dei passeggeri in caso di turbulenza.

P: Lamento, mas não pode colocar qualquer objeto pesado na rede que pode cair na cabeça dos passageiros em caso de turbulência.

S: Lo siento, pero no puede colocar (OR poner) ningún objeto pesado en la rejilla (OR en el portaequipaje), ya que puede caer en la cabeza de los pasajeros en caso de tiempo tormentoso.

216. Will you please put your coat [hat] on the overhead rack?

F: Veuillez mettre votre pardessus [chapeau] dans le filet.

G: Würden Sie bitte Ihren Mantel [Hut] in das Gepäcknetz legen?

I: La prego di mettere il Suo cappotto [cappello] sopra
la rete (OR reticella).

P: Por favor, ponha o seu casaco [chapéu] na rede.

S: ¿Quiere poner su abrigo [sombrero] en la rejilla?

**217. Would you mind holding your coat until all passengers
are seated?**

F: Pouvez-vous garder votre manteau jusqu'à ce que
tous les passagers soient assis?

G: Würden Sie bitte Ihren Mantel halten, bis alle
Passagiere sitzen?

I: Le dispiace tenere il Suo cappotto finchè tutti i
passeggeri siano seduti?

P: Não se importaria de conservar o seu casaco até todos
os passageiros estarem sentados?

S: ¿Le importaría guardar su abrigo hasta que todos los
pasajeros estén sentados?

218. I shall be right back to pick it up.

F: Je vais venir le prendre dans quelques moments.

G: Ich werde sofort zurückkommen, um ihn dann
mitzunehmen.

I: Verrò a prenderlo subito.

P: Voltarei dentro de momentos para levá-lo.

S: Volveré a recogerlo más tarde.

**219. I shall take care of you in just a moment, as soon as all
passengers have been seated.**

F: Je m'occuperai de vous dans un petit instant, dès que
tous les passagers seront assis.

G: Ich werde mich sofort um Sie kümmern, sobald alle
Passagiere sitzen.

I: Mi occuperò di Lei fra qualche minuto, appena tutti i
passeggeri saranno seduti.

P: Atendê-lo-ei dentro de momentos, logo que todos os
passageiros estejam sentados.

S: Me ocuparé de Ud. en un instante, tan pronto como
todos los pasajeros se hayan sentado.

220. May I relieve you of your ———?

F: Puis-je vous débarrasser de votre ———?

G: Darf ich Ihren (Ihre, Ihr) ——— nehmen?

I: Posso togliere (OR prendere) il Suo (la Sua) ———?

P: Posso levar o seu (a sua) ———?

S: ¿Puedo llevar su ———?

221. May I put your ——— on one side?

F: Puis-je mettre de côté votre ———?

G: Darf ich Ihnen den (die, das) ——— abnehmen?

I: Posso mettere da parte il Suo (la Sua) ———?

P: Posso aliviá-lo (TO FEM. aliviá-la) do seu (da sua)
———?

S: ¿Puedo poner al lado su ———?

Cabin Facilities

F: DISPOSITIFS DE LA CABINE

G: KABINENEINRICHTUNGEN

I: ATTREZZATURE DI CABINA

P: INSTALAÇÕES DA CABINA

S: INSTALACIONES DE LA CABINA

222. Here is your reading light switch [your fresh air inlet].

F: Voici l'interrupteur de l'éclairage individuel [une buse
d'air individuelle].

G: Das ist der Knopf für Ihre Leselampe [Ihr Frischluft-
ventil].

I: Questo è l'interruttore della luce per leggere [l'interruttore per l'aria fresca].

P: Aqui está o interruptor da luz de leitura [o renovador de ar].

S: Aquí está su interruptor de luz [su toma de aire fresco].

223. **This is your call button.**

F: Voici votre bouton d'appel.

G: Hier ist Ihr Klingelknopf.

I: Questo è il Suo campanello.

P: Isto é o seu botão de chamada.

S: Este es el timbre de llamada.

224. **If you need something, press this button.**

F: Si vous avez besoin de quelque chose, appuyez sur ce bouton.

G: Wenn Sie etwas brauchen, drücken Sie bitte auf diesen Knopf.

I: Se ha bisogno di qualcosa spinga il bottone.

P: Se precisar de alguma coisa, carregue neste botão.*

S: Si necesita algo, toque este timbre.

225. **The lavatory (OR toilet) is in the rear [in front].**

F: Le lavabo (OR La toilette) se trouve (OR est) à l'arrière [à l'avant].

G: Die Toilette ist hinten [vorne].

I: C'è una toletta dietro [davanti].

P: O lavabo é à rectaguarda [à frente].

S: El lavabo está atrás (OR en el fondo) [en frente].

226. **The ashtray is in the arm rest.**

F: Le cendrier se trouve dans l'accoudoir.

G: Der Aschenbecher ist in der Armlehne.

I: Il portacenere è nel bracciolo.

P: O cinzeiro está no apoio do braço.

S: El cenicero está en el brazo del asiento.

* In Brazil *prema este botão.*

227. This is your tray-table.
  F: Voici votre guide-tablette.
  G: Das ist der Klapptisch für Ihr Tablett.
  I: Questo è il Suo vassoio.
  P: Isto é o seu tabuleiro.
  S: Esta es su mesa-bandeja.

227a. This is your seat belt!
  F: Voici votre ceinture de sécurité (OR sûreté)!
  G: Das ist Ihr Sitzgurt!
  I: Questo è la sua cintura di sicurezza!
  P: Isto é o seu cinto de segurança!
  S: ¡Esto es su cinturón de seguridad!

228. May I show you how to adjust your seat?
  F: Puis-je vous montrer comment ajuster votre siège?
  G: Darf ich Ihnen zeigen, wie Ihr Sitz verstellt wird?
  I: Posso dimostrarLe (OR farLe vedere) come sistemare il Suo sedile?
  P: Posso mostrar-lhe como se regula a sua cadeira?
  S: ¿Puedo mostrarle cómo ajustar su asiento?

229. Now you can recline your seat. You will be more comfortable.
  F: Maintenant vous pouvez incliner votre siège. C'est plus confortable pour vous.
  G: Jetzt können Sie sich zurücklehnen. Das ist bequemer für Sie.
  I: Adesso può reclinare il sedile. Starà più comodo.
  P: Agora pode reclinar a sua cadeira. Fica mais confortável.
  S: Ahora Ud. puede reclinar el asiento. Es más cómodo para Ud.

230. Push the recline control on your arm rest and lean back.
  F: Appuyez sur le bouton de réglage de votre accoudoir et renversez-vous.
  G: Drücken Sie auf den Knopf in der Armlehne und lehnen Sie sich zurück.

I: Prema il pulsante del bracciolo e si appoggi in dietro.
P: Carregue no botão* no apoio do braço e incline-se para trás.
S: Apriete (OR Empuje) el control en el brazo de su asiento y reclínese hacia atrás.

231. Please straighten up your seat!
F: S'il vous plaît, redressez votre siège!
G: Bitte stellen Sie Ihren Sitz nach vorne!
I: Raddrizzi il Suo sedile, per favore!
P: Por favor, endireite a sua cadeira!
S: ¡Por favor, enderezca su asiento!

232. There are water dispensers in both galley areas.
F: Il y a de l'eau potable à votre disposition dans les deux offices de la cabine.
G: Trinkwasser können Sie in beiden Bordküchen bekommen.
I: L'acqua da bere è disponibile nelle due cucinette.
P: Há água para beber em ambas cozinhas.
S: Hay agua para beber en el área de ambas cocinas de abordo.

233. Would you like to have a magazine [a newspaper; a route map; a timetable]?
F: Désirez-vous un magazine [un journal; une carte routière; un horaire]?
G: Möchten Sie eine Zeitschrift [eine Zeitung; eine Streckenkarte; einen Flugplan] haben?
I: Desidera una rivista [un giornale (OR quotidiano); una mappa della rotta; un orario]?
P: Gostaria de ter uma revista [um jornal; um mapa de rota; um horário]?
S: ¿Desea Ud. una revista [un periódico; un mapa de rutas; un horario]?

* In Brazil *Prema o botão.*

234. Your cabin attendant will demonstrate the use of some equipment for your comfort.

F: Votre hôtesse vous expliquera le fonctionnement de certains dispositifs étudiés pour votre confort.

G: Die Stewardeß wird Ihnen den Gebrauch einiger Geräte für Ihre Bequemlichkeit vorführen.

I: La hostess vi mostrerà come usare alcuni accessori per il Vostro conforto (OR per la Vostra comodità).

P: A sua assistente de bordo demonstrará o uso de algum equipamento para o vosso conforto.

S: Su stewardess le enseñará el empleo de algún equipo para su comodidad.

235. In the seat pocket you will find a folder with useful information written in several languages.

F: Dans la poche du fauteuil vous trouverez un dépliant en plusieurs langues contenant des renseignements utiles.

G: In der Sitztasche finden Sie eine mehrsprachige Broschüre mit nützlichen Informationen.

I: Nella tasca del Vostro sedile troverete una guida in diverse lingue con informazioni utili.

P: No bolso de cadeira encontrará uma brochura escrita em várias línguas com úteis informações.

S: En la bolsa del asiento hallará Ud. un folleto escrito en varios idiomas con informaciones útiles.

236. If you read it you will be able to follow the demonstration of some of the equipment in your cabin.

F: En le lisant vous pourrez suivre la démonstration du fonctionnement de quelques dispositifs de votre cabine.

G: Mit Hilfe dieser Broschüre werden Sie der Vorführung einiger Geräte in der Kabine folgen können.

I: Leggendola potrete seguire la dimostrazione di alcuni accessori di cabina.

P: Pela sua leitura pode acompanhar a demonstração de algum equipamento da sua cabina.

S: Leyéndolo Ud. podrá seguir la demostración de algunos equipos de la cabina.

237. The life jacket is located underneath your seat.

F: Le gilet de sauvetage est sous votre siège.

G: Ihre Schwimmveste befindet sich unter Ihrem Sitz.

I: Il salvagente è situato sotto il Vostro sedile.

P: O cinto de salvação está por baixo do seu assento.

S: El chaleco (OR La chaqueta) salvavidas está colocado (colocada) debajo de su asiento.

238. Do not inflate it inside the aircraft.

F: Ne le gonflez pas à l'intérieur de l'appareil.

G: Blasen Sie die Schwimmveste nicht in der Kabine auf.

I: Non gonfiatelo nell'apparecchio.

P: Não o encham dentro do avião.

S: No lo (la) inflen dentro del avión.

239. Life rafts are located in the ceiling of the cabin.

F: Les radeaux (OR canots) de sauvetage se trouvent dans le plafond de la cabine.

G: Schlauchboote sind an der Decke der Kabine vorhanden (OR untergebracht).

I: I canotti di salvataggio sono situati nel tetto (OR nel soffitto) della cabina.

P: Barcos salva-vidas são localizados no teto da cabina.

S: Las balsas salvavidas están colocadas en el techo de la cabina.

240. Hold the oxygen mask over your face.

F: Tenez le masque à oxygène sur votre visage.

G: Ziehen Sie sich die Sauerstoffmaske über das Gesicht.

I: Mettete la maschera d'ossigeno davanti alla Vostra faccia.

P: Coloquem a máscara de oxigénio na sua cara.
S: Pónganse la máscara de oxígeno sobre la cara.

241. **Cover your nose and mouth. Breathe normally.**
    F: Couvrez le nez et la bouche. Respirez normalement.
    G: Halten Sie die Maske über Nase und Mund. Atmen Sie ganz normal.
    I: Coprite il naso e la bocca. Respirate normalmente.
    P: Por favor, cubram o nariz e a boca. Respirem normalmente.
    S: Por favor, cúbranse la nariz y la boca. Respiren normalmente.

242. **The emergency exits are here [there].**
    F: Les sorties de secours sont ici [là-bas].
    G: Hier [Dort] sind die Notausgänge.
    I: Le uscite d'emergenza sono qui [là].
    P: As saídas de emergência são aqui [acolá].
    S: Las salidas de emergencia están aquí [allí].

243. **Here are the airsickness bags.**
    F: Ici se trouvent les sacs vomitoires.
    G: Hier sind die Tüten für den Fall von Luftkrankheit.*
    I: Ecco le borsette in caso di mal d'aria.
    P: Aqui estão os sacos de enjôo.
    S: Aquí están las bolsas en caso de mareo.

244. **Here is a folder with the emergency instructions.**
    F: Voici un dépliant avec les consignes en cas d'urgence.
    G: Hier ist eine Broschüre mit den Anweisungen im Notfall.
    I: EccoLe un opuscolo con le istruzioni di emergenza.
    P: Aqui está um folheto com as instrucções de emergência.
    S: Aquí está un folleto con las instrucciones de emergencia.

* Or, more colloquially, *Hier sind die Spucktüten.*

In-Flight Conversation

F: CONVERSATIONS PENDANT LE VOL
G: GESPRÄCHE WÄHREND DES FLUGES
I: CONVERSAZIONI DURANTE IL VOLO
P: CONVERSAÇÕES DURANTE O VÔO
S: CONVERSACIONES DURANTE EL VUELO

245. **We are going to take off [land] in a few minutes.**
F: Nous allons décoller [atterrir] dans quelques moments.
G: Wir werden in wenigen Minuten starten [landen].
I: Stiamo per decollare [atterrare] fra qualche minuto.
P: Dentro de minutos descolaremos [aterraremos].*
S: Vamos a despegar [aterrizar] dentro de unos minutos.

246. **We are waiting for our clearance from the control tower.**
F: Nous attendons de la tour de contrôle la permission de rouler.
G: Wir warten auf Genehmigung vom Kontrollturm.
I: Attendiamo l'autorizzazione della torre.
P: Estamos a espera de autorização da torre de control.
S: Esperamos que la torre de control nos dé la señal de partida.

247. **Please note the "No Smoking" sign!**
F: S'il vous plaît, observez l'avis: "Défense de fumer."
G: Bitte beachten Sie das Zeichen: "Nicht rauchen."
I: Prego osservare il segnale di non fumare.
P: Favor notar o sinal de "Não fumar!"
S: Por favor, tomen nota del aviso de: "No fumar!"

248. **Fasten your seat belt, please!**
F: Attachez (OR Bouclez) votre ceinture, s'il vous plaît!
G: Bitte schnallen Sie sich an!

* In Brazil *decolaremos [aterrissaremos]*.

I: Prego allacciare la cintura di sicurezza!
P: Por favor, apertem os vossos cintos de segurança!
S: ¡Ajuste* su cinturón de seguridad, por favor!

249. Do you know how to unfasten your seat belt?
F: Savez-vous comment détacher votre ceinture?
G: Können Sie Ihren Sitzgurt lösen?
I: Sapete come slacciare la Sua cintura di sicurezza?
P: Sabe como desapertar o seu cinto de segurança?
S: ¿Sabe Ud. desabrochar (OR zafar) su cinturón de seguridad?

250. May I show you how to do it?
F: Puis-je vous montrer comment le faire?
G: Darf ich Ihnen zeigen, wie es gemacht wird?
I: Posso mostrarLe come fare?
P: Deixe-me mostrar-lhe como deve fazer.
S: ¿Puedo mostrarle cómo sin hacerlo?

251. Is this a non-stop flight?
F: Ce vol est-il direct (OR sans escale)?
G: Ist das ein durchgehender Flug (OR ein Flug ohne Zwischenlandung)?
I: È un volo senza scalo?
P: É este um vôo direito (OR direto)?
S: ¿Es este un vuelo sin escalas?

252. Do we stop at ———?
F: Faisons-nous escale à ———?
G: Machen wir eine Zwischenlandung in ———?
I: Faremo scalo a ———?
P: Paramos em ———?
S: ¿Hacemos escala en ———?

253. What will be the transit time?
F: Quelle sera la durée du transit?
G: Wie lange wird die Aufenthaltszeit dauern?

* In South America *Abroche*.

I: Quanto sarà il tempo di (OR la durata del) transito?
P: Qual será o tempo de trânsito?
S: ¿Cuánto será el tiempo del tránsito?

254. How many stopovers are we going to have?
F: Combien d'escales ferons-nous?
G: Wieviele Zwischenlandungen werden wir machen?
I: Quanti scali faremo?
P: Quantas paragens vamos ter?
S: ¿Cuántas escalas haremos?

255. At what time will we arrive at our destination?
F: À quelle heure arriverons-nous à notre destination?
G: Wann werden wir an unserem Bestimmungsort (OR Zielort) sein?
I: A che ora arriveremo a destinazione?
P: A que horas chegaremos ao nosso destino?
S: ¿A qué hora llegaremos a nuestro destino (OR a nuestra destinación)?

256. At about ——— o'clock in the morning [afternoon; evening].
F: À ——— heures du matin [de l'après-midi; du soir] environ.
G: Ungefähr um ——— Uhr morgens [nachmittags; abends].
I: Verso le ore ——— di mattina [del pomeriggio; di sera].
P: Cerca das ——— horas de manhã [de tarde; de noite].
S: Alrededor de las ——— de la mañana [de la tarde; de la noche].

257. At noon; before [after] midnight.
F: À midi; avant [après] minuit.
G: Mittags; vor [nach] Mitternacht.
I: A mezzogiorno; prima della [dopo la] mezzanotte.
P: Ao meio-dia; antes [depois] de meia-noite.
S: Al mediodía; antes [después] de medianoche.

258. What is our actual flying time?
F: Quelle est la durée du vol?
G: Wie lange dauert die Flugzeit?
I: Quanto sarà il tempo di volo?
P: Qual é o tempo de vôo?
S: ¿Cuál es la duración total del vuelo?

259. Approximately ——— hours and ——— minutes.
F: Approximativement ——— heures et ——— minutes.
G: Ungefähr ——— Stunden und ——— Minuten.
I: Circa ——— ore e ——— minuti.
P: Aproximadamente ——— horas e ——— minutos.
S: Aproximadamente ——— horas y ——— minutos.

260. How far is the city from the airport?
F: Quelle est la distance entre la ville et l'aéroport?
G: Wie weit ist die Stadt vom Flughafen entfernt?
I: Quanto dista la città dall'aeroporto?
P: A que distância fica a cidade do aeroporto?
S: ¿A qué distancia está la ciudad del aeropuerto?

261. Is there a regular bus service between the airport and the city?
F: Y a-t-il un service de cars entre l'aéroport et la ville?
G: Gibt es einen regulären Busverkehr zwischen dem Flughafen und der Stadt?
I: C'è un servizio regolare di autobus fra l'aeroporto e la città?
P: Existe (OR Há) um serviço regular de autocarro entre o aeroporto e a cidade?
S: ¿Hay servicio regular de autobuses entre el aeropuerto y la ciudad?

262. How much does the trip cost?
F: Quel est le prix du trajet?
G: Wieviel kostet die Busfahrt?
I: Qual'è la tariffa del viaggio?
P: Quanto custa a passagem?
S: ¿Cuánto cuesta el viaje?

263. How long does it take from the airport to the city?
    F: Combien de temps faut-il pour aller de l'aéroport à la ville?
    G: Wie lange dauert die Fahrt vom Flughafen in die Stadt?
    I: Quanto tempo ci vuole dall'aeroporto alla città?
    P: Quanto tempo leva do aeroporto à cidade?
    S: ¿Cuánto tiempo dura el trayecto desde el aeropuerto a la ciudad?

264. Please bring me a timetable.
    F: S'il vous plaît, apportez-moi un horaire.
    G: Bitte bringen Sie mir einen Flugplan!
    I: Per cortesia, mi porti un orario.
    P: Por favor, traga-me um horário.
    S: Por favor, tráigame un horario.

265. Will you please check to see if there is a connecting flight tomorrow to ———?
    F: Veuillez vérifier, s'il vous plaît, s'il y a demain un vol en correspondance pour ———.
    G: Würden Sie bitte nachsehen, ob es morgen einen Anschlußflug nach ——— gibt?
    I: Per cortesia, mi controlli se domani c'è un volo in coincidenza per ———.
    P: Favor verificar se há (OR existe) um vôo de ligação amanhã para ———.
    S: ¿Quiere comprobar, por favor, si hay algún vuelo de conexión a ——— para mañana?

266. What is the flight number?
    F: Quel est le numéro du vol?
    G: Wie ist die Flugnummer?
    I: Qual'è il numero del volo?
    P: Qual é o número do vôo?
    S: ¿Cuál es el número de vuelo?

267. What is the check-in time for that flight?

F: À quelle heure doit-on enregistrer pour ce vol?

G: Um wieviel Uhr muß ich mich für diesen Flug melden?

I: A che ora debbo (OR devo) presentarmi per il volo?

P: Qual é a hora de apresentação para esse vôo?

S: ¿Cuál es la hora de presentación para ese vuelo?

268. You will have to be at the airport an hour and a half before departure.

F: Vous devrez être à l'aéroport une heure et demie avant le départ.

G: Sie müssen anderthalb Stunden vor Abflug am Flughafen sein.

I: Deve presentarsi in aeroporto un'ora e mezza prima della partenza.

P: Terá que estar no aeroporto hora e meia antes da partida.

S: Ud. tendrá que estar en el aeropuerto una hora y media antes de la salida.

269. I want to take a connecting flight in the afternoon.

F: Je veux prendre un vol en correspondance dans l'après-midi.

G: Ich möchte einen Anschlußflug am Nachmittag nehmen.

I: Desidero prendere una coincidenza nel pomeriggio.

P: Eu desejo tomar um vôo de ligação de tarde.

S: Quiero tomar un vuelo de conexión por la tarde.

270. The next plane for ———— leaves Friday evening.

F: Le prochain avion pour ———— part vendredi soir.

G: Das nächste Flugzeug nach ———— geht Freitag abend.

I: Il prossimo volo per ———— parte venerdì sera.

P: O próximo avião para ———— parte sexta-feira à tarde.

S: El próximo avión para ———— sale el viernes por la tarde.

271. If you wish you could spend nearly two days at ———.
F: Si vous le désirez, vous pouvez passer presque deux jours à ———.
G: Wenn Sie möchten, könnten Sie fast zwei Tage in ——— verbringen.
I: Se Lei lo desidera, potrebbe stare quasi due giorni a ———.
P: Se desejar, pode passar quase dois dias em ———.
S: Si lo desea, podría pasar casi dos días en ———.

272. That is an excellent idea.
F: C'est une idée excellente.
G: Das ist eine ausgezeichnete Idee.
I: È un'idea eccellente, grazie.
P: Essa é uma ideia excelente.
S: Es una excelente idea.

273. Then I will be able to take a sightseeing tour.
F: De cette façon je pourrai faire le tour de la ville.
G: Dann kann ich eine (Stadt-)Rundfahrt machen.
I: In questo caso posso fare un giro per la città.
P: Então poderei fazer uma volta pela cidade.
S: Entonces podré dar un vistazo a la ciudad.

274. What city are we flying over now?
F: Quelle ville survolons-nous maintenant?
G: Welche Stadt überfliegen wir jetzt?
I: Su quale città stiamo volando ora?
P: Qual é a cidade que estamos sobrevoando?
S: ¿Sobre qué ciudad estamos volando ahora?

275. At what altitude are we flying?
F: À quelle altitude volons-nous?
G: In welcher Höhe fliegen wir?
I: A quale altezza stiamo volando?
P: A que altitude estamos voando?
S: ¿A qué altura volamos?

276. At about ——— feet, that is, about ——— meters.
  F: À ——— pieds, c'est-à-dire ——— mètres environ.
  G: In ungefähr ——— Fuß, das heißt ——— Meter.
  I: A circa ——— piedi, cioè circa ——— metri.
  P: Cerca de ——— pés, isto é aproximadamente ———
       metros.
  S: A unos ——— pies, es decir unos ——— metros.

277. What is the speed of our plane?
  F: Quelle est la vitesse de notre avion?
  G: Wie hoch ist die Geschwindigkeit unserer Maschine?
  I: Qual'è la velocità di questo aereo?
  P: Qual é a velocidade do nosso avião?
  S: ¿Cuál es la velocidad de nuestro avión?

278. About ——— miles, that is, about ——— kilometers, per hour.
  F: À peu près ——— milles, c'est-à-dire à peu près
       ——— kilomètres, par heure.
  G: Ungefähr ——— Meilen, das sind ——— Kilometer,
       in der Stunde.
  I: Circa ——— miglia, cioè ——— chilometri, all'ora.
  P: Cerca de ——— milhas, isto é aproximadamente
       ——— quilómetros, por hora.
  S: Unas ——— millas, es decir ——— kilómetros, por
       hora.

279. Do not worry, you will not miss your connecting flight, since we are on time.
  F: Ne vous inquiétez pas, vous ne manquerez pas la
       correspondance puisque nous sommes à l'heure.
  G: Seien Sie unbesorgt, Sie werden Ihren Anschlußflug
       nicht versäumen, da wir keine Verspätung haben.
  I: Non si preoccupi, non perderà la Sua coincidenza dato
       che siamo in orario.

P: Não se preocupe, não perderá a sua ligação porque vamos dentro do horário.

S: No se preocupe, no perderá su vuelo de conexión ya que no llevamos retraso.

280. **We are ——— minutes [hours] behind schedule because of strong headwinds.**
  F: Nous sommes en retard de ——— minutes [heures] à cause de violents contrevents.
  G: Wir haben eine Verspätung von ——— Minuten [Stunden] wegen starkem Gegenwind.
  I: Abbiamo un ritardo di ——— minuti [ore], causa forti venti contrari.
  P: Nós temos um atrazo de ——— minutos [horas] devido a forte vento contrário.
  S: Llevamos un retraso de ——— minutos [horas] a causa de los fuertes vientos.

281. **Do you think we could make up the lost time?**
  F: Pensez-vous que nous pourrions rattraper le temps perdu?
  G: Glauben Sie, daß wir den Zeitverlust wieder einholen können?
  I: Crede che recupereremo del tempo?
  P: Pensa que poderemos recuperar o tempo perdido?
  S: ¿Cree que podremos recuperar el tiempo perdido?

282. **I do not know, I am going to ask our commander (OR captain).**
  F: Je ne sais pas, je vais le demander au commandant (OR capitaine).
  G: Ich weiß es nicht, ich werde unseren Kapitän fragen.
  I: Non saprei, vado a domandare al comandante.
  P: Não sei, mas vou perguntar ao nosso capitão (OR comandante).
  S: No lo sé, le preguntaré a nuestro capitán (OR comandante).

283. I will let you know as soon as possible.
F: Je vous le ferai savoir dès que possible.
G: Ich werde Ihnen sobald wie möglich Bescheid geben.
I: Glielo farò sapere appena possibile.
P: Dir-lhe-ei logo que seja possível.
S: Se lo comunicaré tan pronto como sea posible.

**284. What will the weather be like when we arrive at
———?**
F: Quel temps fera-t-il lorsque nous arriverons à ———?
G: Wie wird das Wetter bei der Ankunft in ——— sein?
I: Come sarà il tempo all'arrivo a ———?
P: Como estará o tempo na nossa chegada a ———?
S: ¿Qué tiempo hará cuando lleguemos a ———?

**285. According to the last weather forecast at ——— it is
now cold [warm].**
F: D'après les dernières prévisions météorologiques
à ——— il fait froid [chaud] maintenant.
G: Nach der letzten Wettermeldung es ist kalt [warm]
in ———.
I: Secondo l'ultimo bollettino meteorologico a ———
adesso fa (OR è) freddo [caldo].
P: De acordo com a última previsão de tempo em ———
faz frio [calor] agora.
S: Según el último parte (OR boletín) meteorológico,
hace frío [calor] en ———.

**286. It is sunny [it is cloudy; it is windy; it is foggy; it is
humid; it is muggy].**
F: Il fait du soleil [il y a des nuages; il fait du vent; il y
a du brouillard; il y a de l'humidité; il y a beaucoup
d'humidité].
G: Es ist sonnig [es ist bewölkt; es ist windig; es ist
nebelig; es ist feucht; es ist schwül].
I: C'è sole [è nuvoloso; c'è vento; c'è nebbia; fa umido;
fa molto umido].

P: Está sol [está enevoado; está ventoso; está nevoeiro; está húmido; está sufocante].

S: Hay sol [está nublado; hay viento; hay niebla (OR neblina); hay humedad; hay mucha humedad].

287. It is raining [it is snowing; it is drizzling].
F: Il pleut [il neige; il y a une pluie fine].
G: Es regnet [es schneit; es nieselt].
I: Piove [nevica; pioviggina].
P: Está chovendo [está nevando; está chuviscando].
S: Está lloviendo [está nevando; está lloviznando].

288. You will need a raincoat [an umbrella; an overcoat].
F: Vous aurez besoin d'un imperméable [d'un parapluie; d'un pardessus].
G: Sie werden einen Regenmantel [einen Regenschirm; einen Mantel] brauchen.
I: Avrà bisogno di un impermeabile [di un ombrello; di un soprabito].
P: Precisará dum impermeável [dum guarda-chuva; dum sobretudo].
S: Necesitará un impermeable [un paraguas; un abrigo].

289. The temperature is ——— degrees F [C].
F: La température est de ——— degrés F [C].
G: Die Temperatur beträgt ——— Grad F [C].
I: La temperatura è di ——— gradi F [C].
P: A temperatura é ——— graus F [C].
S: La temperatura es de ——— grados F [C].

290. Because of bad weather the flight has been diverted.
F: Notre vol a été dérouté à cause du mauvais temps.
G: Infolge schlechten Wetters ist unser Flug umgeleitet worden.
I: A causa del cattivo tempo l'aereo sarà dirottato.
P: Por causa do mau tempo o nosso vôo divergiu.
S: A causa del mal tiempo nuestro vuelo ha sido desviado.

291. Now we are going to land at ——— instead of ———.
F: Maintenant nous allons atterrir à ——— au lieu
de ———.
G: Wir werden jetzt in ——— statt in ——— landen.
I: Adesso atterreremo a ——— invece di ———.
P: Agora nós vamos aterrar* em ——— em vez
de ———.
S: Ahora vamos a aterrizar en ——— en lugar de ———.

292. Are you comfortable?
F: Vous sentez-vous à votre aise?
G: Fühlen Sie sich wohl?
I: Sta comodo?
P: Está confortável?
S: ¿Se encuentra bien (OR ¿Se siente cómodo)?

293. May I help you?
F: Puis-je vous aider?
G: Kann ich Ihnen behilflich sein?
I: Posso aiutarLa?
P: Posso ajudá-lo (TO FEM. ajudá-la)?
S: ¿Le puedo ayudar?

294. May I show you ———?
F: Puis-je vous montrer ———?
G: Darf ich Ihnen ——— zeigen?
I: Posso mostrarLe ———?
P: Posso mostrar-lhe ———?
S: ¿Me permite enseñarle ———?

295. May I bother (OR trouble) you for a moment?
F: Puis-je vous déranger pour un instant?
G: Darf ich Sie einen Moment stören?
I: Posso disturbarLa per un momento?
P: Posso importuná-lo (TO FEM. importuná-la) por um
momento?
S: ¿Me disculpa (OR ¿Puedo molestarle) un momento?

* In Brazil *aterrissar.*

296. Would you like to have a cigarette?
F: Voudriez-vous une cigarette?
G: Darf ich Ihnen eine Zigarette anbieten?
I: Desidera una sigaretta?
P: Gostaria de fumar um cigarro?
S: ¿Quiere un cigarillo?

297. Thanks, but I am not permitted to smoke while on duty.
F: Je vous en remercie, mais je ne dois pas fumer pendant mon travail.
G: Danke, aber ich darf im Dienst nicht rauchen.
I: Grazie, ma non mi è permesso fumare durante il servizio.
P: Muito obrigado (FEM. obrigada), mas não é permitido fumar durante o serviço.
S: Gracias, no puedo fumar durante mi trabajo.

298. Where is the coatroom (OR cloakroom)?
F: Où est le vestiaire?
G: Wo ist die Garderobe?
I: Dov'è la guardaroba?
P: Onde é o guarda-fato (OR vestiário)?
S: ¿Dónde está el vestuario (OR guardarropa)?

299. Do you have an electric razor?
F: Avez-vous un rasoir électrique?
G: Haben Sie einen elektrischen Rasierapparat?
I: Avete un rasoio elettrico?
P: Tem uma máquina de barbear eléctrica?
S: ¿Tiene una máquina (OR maquinilla) de afeitar eléctrica?

300. Yes, I am going to bring you one.
F: Oui, je vais vous l'apporter.
G: Ja, ich werde Ihnen einen bringen.
I: Sì, Le porterò uno.
P: Sim, vou-lhe trazer uma.
S: Sí, le traeré una.

301. You may use it whenever you wish.
F: Vous pouvez vous en servir quand vous voudrez.
G: Sie können ihn jederzeit benutzen.
I: Può usarlo quando vuole.
P: Pode usá-la quando o desejar.
S: Ud. puede usarla cuando quiera.

302. In the washroom you will find the electrical outlets.
F: Dans le lavabo vous trouverez une prise de courant.
G: Den Stecker finden Sie in den Toiletten.
I: Al gabinetto troverà le prese elettriche.
P: Nos lavabos encontrará a tomada de corrente.
S: En el lavabo Ud. hallará los enchufes eléctricos.

303. How many passengers are on board?
F: Combien de passagers y a-t-il à bord?
G: Wieviel Passagiere sind an Bord?
I: Quanti passeggeri sono a bordo?
P: Quantos passageiros estão a bordo?
S: ¿Cuántos pasajeros hay a bordo?

304. In First Class [Economy Class] we have a total of ———.
F: En Première Classe [Classe Économique] nous avons un total de ———.
G: In der Ersten Klasse [Touristenklasse] haben wir insgesamt ——— Passagiere.
I: In Prima Classe [Classe Economica] abbiamo un totale di ———.
P: Em Primeira Classe [Classe Económica] temos um total de ——— passageiros.
S: En Primera Clase [Clase Económica] tenemos un total de ——— pasajeros.

305. Excuse me, somebody is calling me.
F: Excusez-moi, quelqu'un m'appelle.
G: Entschuldigen Sie bitte, jemand ruft mich.
I: Scusi, qualcuno mi sta chiamando.

P: Desculpe-me, alguém está a chamar-me.*
S: Perdóneme, alguien me llama.

306. Have you any newspapers or magazines?
F: Avez-vous des journaux ou des magazines?
G: Haben Sie Zeitungen oder Zeitschriften?
I: Ha dei giornali o riviste?
P: Tem alguns jornais ou revistas?
S: ¿Tiene Ud. algunos periódicos o revistas?

307. In what languages?
F: En quelles langues?
G: In welchen Sprachen?
I: In che lingue?
P: Em que línguas?
S: ¿En qué idiomas?

308. In English [French, German, Italian, Portuguese, Spanish, Russian, Japanese].
F: En anglais [français, allemand, italien, portuguais, espagnol, russe, japonais].
G: Auf englisch [französisch, deutsch, italienisch, portugiesisch, spanisch, russisch, japanisch].
I: In inglese [francese, tedesco, italiano, portoghese, spagnolo, russo, giapponese].
P: Em inglês [francês, alemão, italiano, português, espanhol, russo, japonês].
S: En inglés [francés, alemán, italiano, portugués, español, ruso, japonés].

309. I cannot close the curtain.
F: Je ne peux pas fermer le rideau.
G: Ich kann den Vorhang nicht zumachen (OR zuziehen, schließen).

---

* In Brazil *alguém me está chamando.*

I: Non posso chiudere la tendina.
P: Não consigo fechar a cortina.
S: No puedo cerrar la cortina.

310. Could you help me?
   F: Pouvez-vous m'aider?
   G: Können Sie mir helfen?
   I: Mi può aiutare?
   P: Pode ajudar-me?
   S: ¿Puede Ud. ayudarme?

311. Certainly! I will be with you in a moment.
   F: Certainement! Je serai à vous dans un instant.
   G: Ja, gewiß! Ich komme in einem Augenblick zurück.
   I: Senz'altro! Sarò da Lei in un minuto!
   P: Certamente! Estarei consigo dentro de momentos.
   S: ¡Cómo no! Estaré con Ud. dentro de un momento.

312. Do you travel frequently?
   F: Voyagez-vous souvent?
   G: Reisen Sie oft (OR häufig)?
   I: Viaggia spesso?
   P: Viaja frequentemente?
   S: ¿Viaja Ud. frecuentemente?

313. I have made many trips this year.
   F: J'ai fait plusieurs voyages cette année.
   G: In diesem Jahre bin ich viel gereist.
   I: Ho fatto molti viaggi quest'anno.
   P: Já fiz várias viajens este ano.
   S: He viajado mucho este año.

314. Have you ever visited ———?
   F: Avez-vous déjà visité ———?
   G: Waren Sie schon einmal in ———?
   I: È mai stato (TO FEM. stata) a ———?
   P: Já visitou ———?
   S: ¿Ha estado alguna vez en ———?

315. **How was the weather during your last flight to ——?**
F: Quel temps a-t-il fait pendant votre dernier vol
   à ——?
G: Wie war das Wetter auf Ihrem letzten Flug nach
   ——?
I: Come era il tempo durante il Suo ultimo volo per
   ——?
P: Como estava o tempo no seu último vôo para ——?
S: ¿Qué tiempo hizo durante su último vuelo para
   ——?

316. **Do you speak ——?**
F: Parlez-vous ——?
G: Sprechen Sie ——?
I: Parla ——?
P: Fala ——?
S: ¿Habla Ud. ——?

317. **I speak a little English [French; German].**
F: Je parle un peu l'anglais [le francais; l'allemand].
G: Ich spreche etwas Englisch [Französisch; Deutsch].
I: Parlo un pochino d'inglese [di francese; di tedesco].
P: Eu falo um pouco de inglês [de francês; de alemão].
S: Hablo un poco de inglés [francés; alemán].

318. **I do not speak it correctly.**
F: Je ne le parle pas correctement.
G: Ich spreche es fehlerhaft.
I: Non lo parlo correttamente.
P: Eu não o falo correctamente.
S: No lo hablo correctamente.

319. **I speak well enough to make myself understood.**
F: Je parle assez bien pour me faire comprendre.
G: Ich spreche gut genug, um mich verständlich zu
   machen.

I: Parlo abbastanza bene da farmi capire.
P: Eu falo-o suficiente para me fazer compreender.
S: Hablo lo suficiente para que me entiendan.

320. Where are you from?
    F: D'où êtes-vous?
    G: Wo sind Sie her?
    I: Di dov'è Lei?
    P: Donde é Vossa Excelência (OR o Senhor, Você)?
    S: De dónde es Ud.?

321. I am from ———.
    F: Je suis de ———.
    G: Ich komme aus ———.
    I: Sono di ———.
    P: Eu sou de ———.
    S: Soy de ———.

322. May I introduce Mister [Mrs.; Miss] ———?
    F: Permettez-moi de vous présenter Monsieur [Madame; Mademoiselle] ———.
    G: Darf ich Ihnen Herrn [Frau; Fräulein] ——— vorstellen?
    I: Permetta che Le presenti il Signor [la Signora; la Signorina] ———.
    P: Permita-me que apresente o Senhor [a Senhora Dona*] ———.
    S: Permítame que le presente al Señor [a la Señora; a la Señorita] ———.

323. How do you do?
    F: Enchanté (FEM. Enchantée).
    G: Es freut mich sehr.
    I: Piacere di fare la Sua conoscenza.
    P: Tenho muito prazer (OR gosto).
    S: Mucho gusto en conocerle.

* In Brazil there is a separate word for "Miss": *a Senhorita.*

324. Who is the gentleman in uniform?

F: Qui est ce monsieur en uniforme?

G: Wer ist der Herr in Uniform?

I: Chi è il Signore in uniforme?

P: Quem é o cavalheiro em uniform?

S: ¿Quién es ese señor en uniforme?

325. He is our commander (OR captain) [one of our officers; our purser].

F: Il est notre commandant (OR capitaine) [un de nos officiers; notre commissaire de bord].

G: Das ist unser Kapitän [einer unserer Offiziere; unser Chefsteward].

I: È il nostro comandante (OR capitano) [uno dei nostri ufficiali; il nostro commissario di bordo].

P: É o nosso capitão (OR comandante) [um de nossos oficiais; o nosso comissário].

S: Es nuestro capitán (OR comandante) [uno de nuestros oficiales; nuestro comisario de abordo (OR nuestro sobrecargo)].

326. How many people does the crew consist of?

F: De combien de personnes se compose l'équipage?

G: Aus wieviel Personen besteht die Besatzung?

I: Di quante persone è composto l'equipaggio?

P: Quantas pessoas tem a tripulação?

S: ¿De cuántas personas se compone la tripulación?

327. I would like to see the cockpit.

F: Je voudrais voir le poste de pilotage.

G: Ich möchte gern die Kanzel besichtigen.

I: Vorrei vedere la cabina di comando.

P: Eu gostaria de ver a cabina de comando (OR o cockpit).

S: Me gustaría ver la cabina de mando.

328. I am sorry, it is not permitted while we are aloft.

F: Je regrette, ce n'est pas permis en vol.

G: Ich bedauere, aber während des Fluges ist das
    verboten.
I: Mi dispiace, ma non è permesso mentre siamo in volo.
P: Lamento, mas não é permitido durante o vôo.
S: Lo siento, pero no es permitido mientras estamos en
    vuelo.

329. You may see it during our next stop.
F: Vous pourrez le visiter pendant notre prochaine escale.
G: Bei der nächsten Zwischenlandung werden Sie sie
    besichtigen können.
I: Potrà vederla durante la prossima fermata.
P: Pode vê-la (vê-lo) durante a nossa próxima paragem.
S: Ud. podrá verla durante nuestra próxima escala.

330. When did you leave ———?
F: Quand avez-vous quitté ———?
G: Wann haben Sie ——— verlassen?
I: Quando è partito (TO FEM. partita) da ———?
P: Quando saiu de ———?
S: ¿Cuándo partió Ud. de ———?

331. I left ——— last Wednesday [last week; last month;
    ——— days ago].
F: Je suis parti (FEM. partie) de ——— mercredi dernier
    [la semaine dernière; le mois dernier; il y a ———
    jours].
G: Ich habe ——— am vorigen Mittwoch [vorige Woche;
    im vorigen (OR vergangenen) Monat; vor ———
    Tagen] verlassen.
I: Sono partito (FEM. partita) da ——— mercoledì
    scorso [la settimana scorsa; il mese scorso; ———
    giorni fa].
P: Saí (OR Parti) de ——— na última quarta-feira [na
    última semana; no último mês; ——— dias atrás].
S: Partí de ——— el miércoles pasado [la semana
    pasada; el mes pasado; hace ——— días].

332. **You speak English fluently [very well; quite well].**
F: Vous parlez couramment [très bien; assez bien] l'anglais.
G: Sie sprechen Englisch fließend [sehr gut; ziemlich gut].
I: Lei parla inglese correntemente [molto bene; piuttosto bene].
P: O Senhor (TO FEM. A Senhora) fala inglês correntemente [muito bem; bastante bem].
S: Ud. habla el inglés corrientemente (OR de corrido) [muy bien; bastante bien].

333. **How long have you been studying French?**
F: Depuis combien de temps étudiez-vous le français?
G: Seit wann lernen Sie Französisch?
I: Per quanto tempo ha studiato il francese?
P: Há quanto tempo estuda o francês?
S: ¿Durante cuánto tiempo ha estudiado Ud. el francés?

334. **Not very long.**
F: Il n'y a pas très longtemps.
G: Noch nicht sehr lange.
I: Non molto.
P: Há pouco tempo.
S: Durante un corto período.

335. **What is your native language?**
F: Quelle est votre langue maternelle?
G: Was ist Ihre Muttersprache?
I: Qual'è la Sua madre lingua?
P: Qual é a sua língua nativa?
S: ¿Cuál es su idioma materno?

336. **Where did you learn German?**
F: Où avez-vous appris l'allemand?
G: Wo haben Sie Deutsch gelernt?

I: Dove ha imparato il tedesco?
P: Onde aprendeu o alemão?
S: ¿Dónde aprendió Ud. el alemán?

337. In (grammar) school [in high school; at college].
F: À l'école [au lycée; à l'université].
G: In der Schule [im Gymnasium; an der Universität].
I: A scuola [al liceo; all'università].
P: Na escola [no liceu; na universidade].
S: En la escuela [en el colegio; en la Universidad].

338. In a language laboratory, with the help of tape recorders and records.
F: Au laboratoire de langues, à l'aide des magnétophones et des disques.
G: In dem Sprachlaboratorium, mit Hilfe von Tonbandgeräten und Schallplatten.
I: Nel laboratorio di lingue, con l'aiuto di registratori a nastro e di dischi.
P: No laboratório de línguas, com ajuda de fitas gravadas e discos.
S: En el laboratorio de idiomas, con ayuda de cintas magnetofónicas y discos.

339. I spent several months in ———.
F: J'ai passé plusieurs mois en (à, au, aux) ———.
G: Ich habe einige Monate in ——— verbracht.
I: Sono stato (FEM. stata) parecchi mesi in ———.
P: Passei vários meses em ———.
S: Pasé varios meses en ———.

340. I learned Italian at home from my parents.
F: Mes parents m'ont enseigné l'italien chez moi.
G: Ich habe Italienisch zu Hause von meinen Eltern gelernt.
I: Ho imparato l'italiano a casa dai miei genitori.
P: Aprendi o italiano em casa com os meus pais.
S: Aprendí el italiano en casa de mis padres.

341. I had a private teacher.
F: J'ai eu un professeur privé.
G: Ich hatte einen Privatlehrer.
I: Ho avuto un maestro privato.
P: Tive um professor particular.
S: Tuve un professor privado.

342. How do you say ——— in Portuguese?
F: Comment dit-on ——— en portugais?
G: Wie sagt man ——— auf portugiesisch?
I: Come si dice ——— in portoghese?
P: Como diz-se ——— em português?
S: ¿Cómo se dice ——— en portugués?

343. Excuse me, I did not understand you completely.
F: Excusez-moi, je ne vous ai pas compris parfaitement.
G: Verzeihung, ich habe Sie nicht richtig verstanden.
I: Mi scusi, non ho capito bene.
P: Desculpe-me, mas não percebi completamente.
S: Perdón, no le he comprendido del todo.

344. You speak too fast for me. Please speak more slowly.
F: Vous parlez trop vite pour moi. Parlez plus lentement, s'il vous plaît.
G: Sie sprechen zu schnell für mich. Sprechen Sie bitte etwas langsamer!
I: Lei parla troppo velocemente per me. Per favore, parli più lentamente (OR adagio).
P: Fala muito depressa para mim. Por favor, fale mais devagar!
S: Ud. habla demasiado rápido (OR de prisa) para mí. ¡Por favor, hable más despacio!

345. I know that I have to improve my pronunciation.
F: Je sais que je dois perfectionner ma prononciation.
G: Ich weiß, daß ich meine Aussprache noch verbessern muß.
I: So che devo migliorare la mia pronuncia.

P: Eu sei que tenho de melhorar a minha pronúncia.
S: Sé que debo mejorar mi pronunciación.

346. I will have to increase my vocabulary.
F: Il faut que j'augmente mon vocabulaire.
G: Ich muß meinen Wortschatz noch erweitern.
I: Devo arricchire il mio vocabolario.
P: Terei que aumentar o meu vocabulário.
S: Tendré que aumentar mi vocabulario.

347. I always try to speak in Spanish.
F: Je tâche toujours de parler en espagnol.
G: Ich versuche immer, Spanisch zu sprechen.
I: Cerco sempre di parlare in spagnolo.
P: Eu tento sempre falar espanhol.
S: Siempre intento hablar español.

348. I take advantage of every opportunity to speak French [read French books; see French films; listen to French records and tapes].
F: Je profite de toutes les occasions de parler français [lire des livres en français; voir des films en français; écouter des disques et des bandes magnétiques en français].
G: Ich benütze jede Gelegenheit, um Französisch zu sprechen [französische Bücher zu lesen; französische Filme zu sehen; französische Schallplatten und Tonbandaufnahmen zu hören].
I: Approfitto di ogni opportunità per parlare francese [leggere libri francesi; vedere dei film in francese; ascoltare dischi e registrazioni in francese].
P: Eu aproveito todas as oportunidades para falar francês [ler livros franceses; ver filmes franceses; ouvir discos e gravações em francês].
S: Siempre aprovecho cada oportunidad para hablar francés [leer libros en francés; ver películas (OR cintas) en francés; escuchar discos y cintas (magnéticas) grabadas en francés].

349. Did you understand what I was saying?
F: Avez-vous compris ce que j'ai dit?
G: Haben Sie verstanden, was ich gesagt habe?
I: Ha capito quello che ho detto?
P: Compreendeu (OR Percebeu) o que eu disse?
S: ¿Ha entendido (OR comprendido) Ud. lo que he dicho?

350. Do you understand what you are reading?
F: Comprenez-vous ce que vous lisez?
G: Verstehen Sie, was Sie lesen?
I: Capisce quello che sta leggendo?
P: Compreende o que está a ler?*
S: ¿Entiende (OR Comprende) Ud. lo que está leyendo?

351. I do not understand this sentence [this word; the question; the answer].
F: Je ne comprends pas cette phrase [ce mot; la question; la réponse].
G: Diesen Satz [dieses Wort; die Frage; die Antwort] verstehe ich nicht.
I: Non capisco questa frase [questa parola; la domanda; la risposta].
P: Eu não compreendo (OR percebo) esta frase [esta palavra; a pergunta; a resposta].
S: No comprendo esta frase [esta palabra; la pregunta; la respuesta].

352. Can you explain this to me?
F: Pouvez-vous m'expliquer ceci?
G: Können Sie mir das erklären?
I: Può spiegarmi questo?
P: Pode-me explicar isto?
S: ¿Me puede explicar esto?

353. I will try to translate this for you.
F: Je vais essayer de vous traduire ceci.
G: Ich werde versuchen, das für Sie zu übersetzen.

* In Brazil *está lendo.*

I: Cercherò di tradurLe questo.
P: Tentarei traduzir-lhe isto.
S: Trataré de traducirle esto a Ud.

354. Have you a dictionary by any chance?
    F: Avez-vous par hasard un dictionnaire?
    G: Haben Sie zufällig ein Wörterbuch?
    I: Ha per caso un dizionario?
    P: Tem por acaso um dicionário?
    S: ¿Tiene Ud. por casualidad un diccionario?

355. Does anyone here speak English?
    F: Y a-t-il quelqu'un qui parle anglais?
    G: Spricht hier irgendjemand Englisch?
    I: C'è qualcuno qui che parla inglese?
    P: Há alguém aqui que fale inglês?
    S: ¿Hay alguien aquí que hable inglés?

356. I speak it a little.
    F: Je le parle un peu.
    G: Ich kann es ein wenig.
    I: Io lo parlo un pochino.
    P: Eu falo um pouco.
    S: Yo lo hablo un poco.

357. I can understand everything, but I cannot speak it.
    F: Je peux tout comprendre, mais je ne le parle pas.
    G: Ich kann alles verstehen, aber ich spreche es nicht.
    I: Capisco tutto, ma non posso parlare.
    P: Eu compreendo tudo, mas não posso falar.
    S: Puedo entenderlo todo, pero no puedo hablarlo.

358. I have forgotten that word.
    F: J'ai oublié ce mot.
    G: Ich habe das Wort vergessen.
    I: Ho dimenticato questa parola.
    P: Eu esqueci-me dessa palavra.
    S: He olvidado esta palabra.

359. I do not remember.
F: Je ne me souviens pas (OR Je ne me rappelle pas).
G: Ich kann mich nicht erinnern.
I: Non mi ricordo.
P: Eu não me lembro.
S: No lo recuerdo.

360. I am going to ask the other stewardess.
F: Je vais le demander à l'autre hôtesse.
G: Ich werde die andere Stewardeß fragen.
I: Lo domando all'altra hostess.
P: Vou perguntar à outra hospedeira.*
S: Voy a preguntar a la otra stewardess.

361. Do you have much trouble understanding me?
F: Avez-vous beaucoup de difficulté à me comprendre?
G: Haben Sie Schwierigkeiten, mich zu verstehen?
I: È molto difficile per Lei capirmi?
P: É-lhe muito difícil perceber-me?
S: ¿Le es muy difícil a Ud. el entenderme?

362. No, on the contrary, it is very easy.
F: Non, au contraire, c'est très facile.
G: Nein, im Gegenteil, es geht sehr gut.
I: No, al contrario, è molto facile.
P: Não, pelo contrário, é muito fácil.
S: No, al contrario, es muy fácil.

363. I am not feeling well.
F: Je ne me sens pas bien.
G: Ich fühle mich nicht wohl.
I: Non mi sento bene.
P: Eu não me sinto bem.
S: No me siento bien.

* In Brazil *aeromoça.*

364. Do you have some tablets for airsickness?
F: Avez-vous des pilules contre le mal d'avion?
G: Haben Sie Tabletten gegen Luftkrankheit?
I: Ha delle pillole per il mal d'aria?
P: Tem algum comprimido para o enjôo?
S: ¿Tiene Ud. algunas tabletas (OR píldoras, pastillas) contra el mal de vuelo?

365. I have a headache.
F: J'ai mal à la tête.
G: Ich habe Kopfschmerzen.
I: Ho mal di testa.
P: Eu tenho dor de cabeça.
S: Tengo dolor de cabeza.

366. I have a buzzing in my ears.
F: Mes oreilles bourdonnent.
G: Ich habe Ohrensausen.
I: Ho un ronzio nelle orecchie.
P: Eu tenho um zumbido nos meus ouvidos.
S: Tengo zumbidos en los oídos.

367. I am very tired. I want to sleep.
F: Je suis très fatigué (FEM. fatiguée). Je veux dormir.
G: Ich bin sehr müde. Ich möchte schlafen.
I: Sono molto stanco (FEM. stanca). Vorrei dormire.
P: Estou muito cansado (FEM. cansada). Gostava de dormir.
S: Estoy muy cansado (FEM. cansada). Deseo dormir.

368. Here is a pillow [a blanket] for you.
F: Voici un oreiller [une couverture] pour vous.
G: Hier ist ein Kissen [eine Decke] für Sie!
I: Ecco un cuscino [una coperta] per Lei!
P: Aqui tem uma almofada [um cobertor] para si!
S: Aquí hay una almohada [una manta (OR frazada)] para Ud.

369. Would you please turn off the light?

F: Voulez-vous, s'il vous plaît, éteindre la lumière?

G: Würden Sie bitte das Licht ausmachen (OR ausschalten)?

I: Per favore, spenga la luce!

P: Fazia o favor de apagar a luz?

S: ¡Por favor, apague la luz!

370. Please wake me up at ——— o'clock.

F: Veuillez me réveiller à ——— heures.

G: Wecken Sie mich bitte um ——— Uhr!

I: Per favore, mi svegli alle ———.

P: Por favor, acorde-me às ——— horas!

S: ¡Por favor, despiérteme a las ———!

371. I shall not forget to wake you up at ———.

F: Je n'oublierai pas de vous réveiller à ——— heures.

G: Ich werde nicht vergessen, Sie um ——— Uhr zu wecken.

I: Non dimenticherò di svegliarLa alle ———.

P: Não me esquecerei de o (TO FEM. a) acordar às ——— horas.

S: No me olvidaré despertarle a las ———.

372. Did you sleep well?

F: Avez-vous bien dormi?

G: Haben Sie gut geschlafen?

I: Ha dormito bene?

P: Dormiu bem?

S: ¿Durmió bien?

373. Unfortunately I could not sleep.

F: Malheureusement je n'ai pas pu dormir.

G: Leider konnte ich nicht schlafen.

I: Purtroppo non ho potuto dormire.

P: Infelizmente não consegui (OR pude) dormir.

S: Desgraciadamente no pude dormir.

374. What is the date today?
F: Quelle est la date aujourd'hui?
G: Den wievielten haben wir heute?
I: Quanti ne abbiamo oggi?
P: A quantos estamos hoje?
S: ¿Qué fecha es hoy?

375. March nineteenth. April first.
F: Le dix-neuf mars. Le premier avril.
G: Den neunzehnten März. Den ersten April.
I: Il diciannove marzo. Il primo aprile.
P: O dezenove de março. O primeiro de abril.
S: El diez y nueve de marzo. El primero de abril.

376. What day of the week is it?
F: Quel jour sommes-nous?
G: Welcher Tage ist heute?
I: Che giorno è oggi?
P: Que dia é hoje?
S: ¿Qué día de la semana es hoy?

377. Today is Wednesday.
F: C'est aujourd'hui mercredi.
G: Heute ist Mittwoch.
I: Oggi è mercoledì.
P: Hoje é quarta-feira.
S: Hoy es miércoles.

378. This week; next month; last year.
F: Cette semaine; le mois prochain; l'année dernière.
G: Diese Woche; nächsten Monat; voriges Jahr.
I: Questa settimana; il mese prossimo; l'anno scorso
(OR passato).
P: Esta semana; o próximo mês (OR o mês seguinte); o
ano passado.
S: Esta semana; el próximo mes; el año pasado.

379. In spring; in summer; in the fall (OR autumn); in winter.
F: Au printemps; en été; en automne; en hiver.
G: Im Frühling; im Sommer; im Herbst; im Winter.
I: Durante la primavera; nell'estate; nell'autunno; nell'inverno.
P: Na primavera; no verão; no outono; no inverno.
S: En primavera; en verano; en otoño; en invierno.

380. What is your favorite season?
F: Quelle est votre saison favorite (OR préférée)?
G: Welche Jahreszeit haben Sie am liebsten?
I:. Quale stagione preferisce?
P: Qual é a sua estação preferida?
S: ¿Cuál es su estación favorita (OR preferida)?

381. Do you like swimming [do you like ice skating; do you like skiing; do you like horseback riding?]
F: Aimez-vous nager [aimez-vous patiner; aimez-vous faire du ski; aimez-vous monter à cheval]?
G: Schwimmen Sie gerne [laufen Sie gerne Schlittschuh; laufen Sie gerne Schi (OR Ski); reiten Sie gerne]?
I: Le piace il nuoto [le piace il pattinaggio sul ghiaccio; le piace lo sci; le piace l'equitazione]?
P: Gosta de nadar [gosta da patinagem no gelo; gosta de esquiar; gosta da equitação]?
S: ¿Le gusta Ud. nadar [le gusta patinar sobre hielo; le gusta esquiar; le gusta montar a caballo]?

382. I prefer playing tennis [golf].
F: Je préfère jouer au tennis [au golf].
G: Ich spiele lieber Tennis [Golf].
I: Preferisco giocare a tennis [a golf].
P: Eu prefiro jogar ténis [golfe].
S: Prefiero jugar al tenis [al golf].

383. Tell me, please, where can I buy duty-free liquor?
F: Dites-moi, s'il vous plaît, où puis-je acheter des liqueurs détaxées?

G: Können Sie mir bitte sagen, wo ich zollfreie Getränke kaufen kann?

I: Mi dica, per favore, dove posso comprare liquori esenti da tasse doganali?

P: Diga-me, por favor, onde posso comprar bebidas isentas da taxa?

S: Dígame, por favor, ¿dónde puedo comprar bebidas libres (or exentas) de impuesto?

384. Most airports have their own duty-free stores.

F: La plupart des aéroports ont leurs propres boutiques détaxées.

G: Die meisten Flughäfen haben ihre eigenen zollfreien Läden.

I: Quasi tutti gli aeroporti hanno un magazzino per merce esente da tasse doganali.

P: A maioria dos aeroportos tem os seus armazéns de isenção de taxas.

S: La mayoría de los aeropuertos tienen tiendas donde venden libre de impuestos.

385. To an intoxicated passenger: I am sorry, Sir, but we are not allowed to serve you any more drinks.

F: *À un passager enivré:* Je suis désolé (FEM. désolée), Monsieur, mais nous ne pouvons plus vous servir à boire.

G: *Zu einem betrunkenen Passagier:* Es tut mir leid, mein Herr, aber wir dürfen Ihnen keine Getränke mehr servieren.

I: *Ad un passeggero ubriaco:* Mi dispiace, Signore, ma non possiamo servirLe altri liquori.

P: *Para um passageiro embriagado:* Lamento, mas não nos é permitido servir-lhe mais bebidas.

S: *A un pasajero ebrio:* Lo siento, pero no podemos servirle más bebidas.

386. We have to take the bottle away from you.

F: Nous devons vous enlever cette bouteille.

G: Wir müssen Ihnen die Flasche wegnehmen.

I: Dobbiamo portare via la bottiglia.

P: Nós temos que retirar-lhe a garrafa.

S: Tenemos que retirarle la botella.

387. *To a passenger smoking a cigar:* Would you be kind enough to refrain from smoking the cigar?

F: *À un passager fumant un cigare:* Ayez la bonté de cesser de fumer le cigare.

G: *Zu einem zigarrerauchenden Passagier:* Würden Sie so freundlich sein, das Zigarrenrauchen einzustellen?

I: *Ad un passaggero che fuma un sigaro:* Vuole essere così gentile di non fumare il sigaro?

P: *Para um passageiro fumando charuto:* Agradeceríamos se não fumasse charuto.

S: *A un pasajero fumando un cigarro* (OR *puro*)*:* ¿Tendría la bondad de abstenerse de fumar el cigarro (OR puro)?

388. You may go to the back and smoke just one.

F: Vous pouvez aller à l'arrière et en fumer un seulement.

G: Sie können nach hinten gehen und *eine* Zigarre rauchen.

I: Può andare dietro a fumarne uno soltanto.

P: Pode ir para a rectaguarda e fumar sòmente um charuto.

S: Puede ir al fondo y ahí puede fumar uno.

389. The smoke in the air system can be nauseating to passengers who have a weak stomach.

F: La fumée du cigare avec le systeme d'air conditionné peut incommoder les passagers ayant un estomac délicat.

G: Der Rauch in der Luft kann Übelkeit bei den Passagieren hervorrufen, die einen empfindlichen Magen haben.

I: Il fumo nell'aria può nauseare i passeggeri che soffrono di stomaco.

P: O fumo no sistema de ventilação pode ser nausea-
bundo para os passageiros com estômago sensível.

S: El humo en el aire puede causar malestar a otros
pasajeros con estómago delicado.

390. Thanks very much for your cooperation, Sir.

F: Je vous remercie beaucoup de votre compréhension,
Monsieur!

G: Vielen Dank für Ihr Verständnis.

I: Grazie per la Sua cooperazione, Signore.

P: Muito obrigado (FEM. obrigada) pela sua cooperação.

S: ¡Gracias por su comprensión, Señor!

**391. I am very sorry, but pipe smoking is forbidden by the
international regulations.**

F: Je suis désolé (FEM. désolée), mais les règlements
internationaux interdisent de fumer la pipe.

G: Es tut mir leid, aber das Pfeiferauchen ist nach den
internationalen Vorschriften verboten.

I: Mi dispiace, ma il fumare la pipa è vietato da regolamenti internazionali.

P: Lamento imenso, mas os regulamentos internacionais
proibem fumar cachimbo.

S: Lo siento, pero el fumar en pipa está prohibido por
reglamentos internacionales.

392. Sit here and chat with me!

F: Asseyez-vous ici et bavardez un peu avec moi!

G: Setzen Sie sich bitte hierher und unterhalten Sie
sich ein bißchen mit mir!

I: Perchè non si siede qui e chiacchera con me?

P: Porque não se senta aqui e conversa um pouco comigo?

S: Siéntase por favor y charle conmigo.

393. I would like to, but I have a few more things to do.

F: Je le voudrais bien, mais j'ai encore quelque chose à
faire.

G: Ich würde es gern tun, aber ich muß noch einige Sachen erledigen.

I: Mi piacerebbe, ma ho ancora da fare.

P: Eu gostaria, mas tenho algumas coisas mais para fazer.

S: Me gustaría hacerlo, pero tengo unas otras cosas que hacer.

394. Is this your first flight with us?

F: Est-ce votre premier vol avec nous?

G: Ist dies Ihr erster Flug mit uns?

I: È questo il Suo primo volo con noi?

P: É este o seu primeiro vôo connosco?*

S: ¿Es la primera vez que vuela con nosotros?

395. I hope you have enjoyed this flight so far.

F: J'espère que vous soyez satisfait (TO FEM. satisfaite) de ce vol jusqu'à présent.

G: Ich hoffe, daß dieser Flug Ihnen bis jetzt gefallen hat.

I: Spero che fino ad ora Le sia piacuto il volo.

P: Espero que o vôo até agora lhe tenha sido agradável.

S: Espero que esté disfrutando su viaje.

396. Certainly, I have enjoyed it, except that I feel so nervous because this plane is shaking.

F: Certainement, je suis satisfait (FEM. satisfaite), bien que les secousses de l'appareil m'inquiètent.

G: Es hat mir schon gefallen, nur bin ich so nervös, weil diese Maschine rüttelt.

I: Certamente mi è piacuto, eccetto che sono molto nervoso (FEM. nervosa) perchè l'aereo si agita.

P: Certamente que eu tenho gostado, contudo sinto-me muito nervoso (FEM. nervosa) porque este avião tem abanado.

S: Ciertamente lo estoy disfrutando, salvo que estoy siempre nervioso (FEM. nerviosa) porque el avión se sacude.

---

* In Brazil *conosco*.

397. I would not worry about that. It is just a mild turbulence.
F: Cela ne m'inquièterait pas, ce sont des secousses normales.
G: Ich würde mich darüber nicht aufregen, es ist nur eine leichte Turbulenz.
I: Non si preoccupi per questo, è solo una leggera turbolenza.
P: Eu não me preocuparia porque é sòmente uma turbulência ligeira.
S: No me preocuparía, ya que es una pequeña turbulencia en el aire.

398. It is very much like rough weather on the ocean, except that we cannot see the waves.
F: C'est à peu près comme du mauvais temps sur l'océan, sauf que nous ne voyons pas les vagues.
G: Es ist ungefähr so wie bei stürmischem Wetter auf dem Meer, nur daß wir die Wellen nicht sehen können.
I: È simile al cattivo tempo sull'oceano, eccetto che non possiamo vedere le onde.
P: É muito parecido com o mau tempo no oceano, excepto que não podemos ver as ondas.
S: Este fenómeno es parecido al oleaje en el océano, salvo que no vemos las olas.

399. *To an elderly passenger:* Are you going to visit your family?
F: *À un passager âgé:* Allez-vous visiter votre famille ?
G: *Zu einem älteren Fluggast:* Wollen Sie Ihre Familie besuchen ?
I: *Ad un passeggero anziano:* Va visitare la famiglia ?
P: *Para um passageiro de idade:* Vai visitar a sua família ?
S: *A una persona de edad:* ¿Va Ud. a visitar a sus familiares ?

400. How long has it been since you have seen your family?
F: Depuis combien de temps n'avez-vous pas vu votre famille?
G: Wie lange ist es her, daß Sie Ihre Familie nicht mehr gesehen haben?
I: Quant'è che non vede la Sua famiglia?
P: Há quanto tempo não vê a sua família?
S: ¿Cuánto tiempo hace que no ha visto a sus familiares?

401. The last time I saw them was ten years ago.
F: Je les ai vus la dernière fois il y a dix ans.
G: Ich habe sie vor zehn Jahren zum letzten Mal gesehen.
I: L'ultima volta che ho visto i miei familiari è stato dieci anni fa.
P: A última vez que os vi foi há dez anos.
S: Los ví por última vez hace diez años.

402. Do they speak German?
F: Parlent-ils allemand?
G: Sprechen sie Deutsch?
I: Parlano tedesco?
P: Falam eles alemão?
S: ¿Hablan ellos alemán?

403. Yes, quite well.
F: Oui, assez bien.
G: Ja, ganz gut.
I: Sì, piuttosto bene.
P: Sim, bastante bem.
S: Sí, bastante bien.

404. Are you going to visit New York [Paris]?
F: Allez-vous visiter New York [Paris]?
G: Werden Sie New York [Paris] besichtigen?
I: Visiterà Nuova York [Parigi]?
P: Vai visitar Nova Iorque [Paris]?
S: ¿Va Ud. a visitar Nueva York [París]?

405. I am going to ———, then continuing to ——— and then returning by way of ———.
F: Je vais aller à ———, puis continuer vers ——— et ensuite retourner par ———.
G: Ich gehe nach ———, dann weiter nach ——— und dann zurück über ———.
I: Vado a ———, poi continuo per ——— e ritorno via ———.
P: Eu vou para ———, depois continuo para ——— e por fim regresso via ———.
S: Voy a ———, luego continuaré a ———, regresando vía (OR por) ———.

406. What days do you work and what days are you off?
F: Quels jours travaillez-vous et quels jours vous reposez-vous?
G: An welchen Tagen arbeiten Sie und welche Tage haben Sie frei?
I: In quali giorni lavora e in quali giorni riposa?
P: Em que dias trabalha e em que dias descansa?
S: ¿En qué días trabaja Ud. y en qué días descansa Ud.?

407. That depends on our monthly schedule.
F: Cela dépend de notre horaire mensuel.
G: Das hängt von unserem monatlichen Flugplan ab.
I: Dipende dal nostro orario mensile.
P: Isso depende do nosso horário mensal.
S: Eso depende de nuestro plan mensual de vuelo.

408. How many hours do you work on a flight?
F: Combien d'heures travaillez-vous en vol?
G: Wieviele Stunden arbeiten Sie auf einem Flug?
I: Quante ore lavora per volo?
P: Quantas horas trabalha num vôo?
S: ¿Cuántas horas trabaja Ud. en un vuelo?

409. We are always at the disposal of our passengers.
F: Nous sommes toujours à la disposition de nos passagers.
G: Wir stehen unseren Passagieren immer zur Verfügung.
I: Siamo sempre a disposizione dei nostri passeggeri.
P: Estamos sempre à disposição dos nossos passageiros.
S: Siempre estamos a la disposición de nuestros pasajeros.

410. We never leave them completely unattended.
F: Nous ne les laissons jamais seuls.
G: Wir lassen sie nie ganz alleine.
I: Non li lasciamo mai completamente soli.
P: Nós nunca os deixamos completamente sós.
S: Nunca les dejamos completamente solos.

411. Consequently, we take turns eating.
F: En conséquence nous mangeons à tour de rôle.
G: Demzufolge wechseln wir uns im Essen ab.
I: Di conseguenza, mangiamo a turno.
P: Em consequência, nós comemos por turnos.
S: Por lo tanto, turnamos para comer.

412. Because of turbulence we are compelled to put on the seat belt sign.
F: À cause de la turbulence nous sommes obligés d'allumer le signal d'attacher vos ceintures.
G: Wegen Turbulenz müssen wir das Zeichen zum Anschnallen einschalten.
I: A causa della turbolenza dobbiamo accendere il segnale per allacciare le cinture di sicurezza.
P: Em resultado de turbulência somos forçados a iluminar o sinal de pôr os cintos de segurança.
S: A causa del temporal (OR de la turbulencia) debemos encender* la señal de abrochar sus cinturones de seguridad.

* In South America *poner*.

413. You should not be afraid.
F: Vous ne devez pas vous inquiéter.
G: Sie brauchen keine Angst zu haben.
I: Non deve avere paura.
P: Não deve ter medo.
S: ¡No tema (OR ¡No tenga miedo)!

414. You will not fall out of the seat, because you have the seat belt on.
F: Votre ceinture de sécurité vous empêchera de tomber de votre siège.
G: Sie werden nicht aus dem Sitz fallen, da Sie den Sitzgurt anhaben.
I: Non cadrà dal posto perchè ha la cintura di sicurezza.
P: Não cairá do assento porque tem o cinto de segurança posto.
S: No se caerá del asiento porque tiene puesto el cinturón de seguridad.

415. Any noises that you hear are routine.
F: Tous les bruits que vous entendez sont normaux.
G: Irgendwelche Geräusche, die Sie hören, sind normal.
I: I rumori che sente sono normali.
P: Qualquer barulho que ouça é normal.
S: Los ruidos que oye son de rutina.

416. What is wrong? Is anything going to happen?
F: Que se passe-t-il? Va-t-il arriver quelque chose?
G: Was ist los? Wird etwas passieren?
I: Cosa c'è? Succederà qualcosa?
P: O que é que está mal? Vai suceder alguma coisa?
S: ¿Qué ocurre (OR ¿Qué pasa)? ¿Va a suceder algo?

417. There is nothing to worry about.
F: Il n'y a pas lieu de s'inquiéter.
G: Sie brauchen sich keine Sorgen zu machen.

I: Non c'è da preoccuparsi.
P: Não há nada que se preocupar.
S: No hay por qué preocuparse.

418. We are going through clear-air turbulence; therefore you do not see any clouds.

F: Nous passons une turbulence de clair air; c'est pourquoi vous ne voyez aucun nuage.
G: Wir fliegen durch Turbulenz in klarer Luft, darum sehen Sie keine Wolken.
I: Attraversiamo turbolenza in cielo sereno, quindi non si vedono nubi.
P: Nos vamos através de turbulência em céu limpo, por tanto não vê qualquer nuvem.
S: Atravesamos un ligero temporal pese al cielo despejado, por eso no ve ninguna nube.

419. I see the wings moving. Are they going to fall off?

F: Je vois les ailes qui bougent. Vont-elles tomber?
G: Ich sehe, daß sich die Tragflächen bewegen. Werden sie abfallen?
I: Vedo le ali muoversi. Cadranno?
P: Eu vejo as asas moverem-se. Irão cair?
S: Veo que se mueven las alas. ¿Se van a caer?

420. The wings of an aircraft are designed to be flexible.

F: Les ailes d'un avion sont prévues flexibles.
G: Die Maschine hat bewegliche Tragflächen.
I: Le ali degli aerei sono flessibili.
P: As asas de um avião são disenhadas para serem flexíveis.
S: Las alas del avión han sido diseñadas para que sean flexibles.

421. Please have no fear. The pilots have everything under control.

F: Ne vous inquiétez pas, s'il vous plaît. L'équipage a le contrôle absolu de l'appareil.

G: Bitte haben Sie keine Angst. Die Piloten haben alles unter Kontrolle.

I: Non abbia paura. I piloti hanno tutto sotto controllo.

P: Por favor, não tenha receio. Os pilotos têm tudo controlado.

S: Por favor, no tema, ya que los pilotos tienen todo bajo control.

422. I want to change my seat.

F: Je veux changer de siège.

G: Ich möchte meinen Platz wechseln.

I: Voglio cambiare il posto.

P: Eu quero mudar de lugar.

S: Deseo cambiar de asiento.

423. The passenger behind me is constantly singing.

F: Le passager derrière moi chante sans interruption.

G: Der Passagier hinter mir singt unaufhörlich.

I: Il passaggero dietro di me canta continuamente.

P: O passageiro atrás de mim canta constantemente.

S: El pasajero detrás mí canta continuamente.

424. I have been traveling a lot the last few days and I am very tired.

F: J'ai beaucoup voyagé ces derniers jours et je suis très fatigué (FEM. fatiguée).

G: Ich bin in den letzten Tagen ständig unterwegs gewesen und ich bin sehr müde.

I: Ho viaggiato molto in questi giorni e sono molto stanco (FEM. stanca).

P: Tenho viajado muito estes dias e estou muito cansado (FEM. cansada).

S: He viajado mucho durante estos días y estoy muy cansado (FEM. cansada).

425. Sir, could you kindly refrain from singing so loudly?

F: Monsieur, pourriez-vous, s'il vous plaît, vous abstenir de chanter si fort?